Photoshop 5
Type Magic

Photoshop 5 Type Magic

BY GREG SIMSIC

Photoshop 5 Type Magic

International Standard Book Number: 156830-465-x

Library of Congress Catalog Card Number: 98-84021

Printed in the United States of America

First Printing: June, 1998

00 99 98   4   3   2   1

Interpretation of the printing code: the rightmost double-digit number is the year of the book's printing; the rightmost single-digit number is the number of the book's printing. For example, a printing code of 95-1 shows that the first printing of the book occurred in 1995.

This book was produced digitally by Macmillan Computer Publishing and manufactured using computer-to-plate technology (a film-less process) by GAC/Shepard Poorman, Indianapolis, Indiana.

Trademarks

iv

Publisher
Jordan Gold

Executive and Development Editor
Beth Millett

Managing Editor
Brice Gosnell

Software Development Specialist
Adam Swetnam

Project Editor
Kevin Laseau

Copy Editor
San Dee Phillips

Technical Editor
Kate Binder

Cover Designer
Aren Howell

Book Designer
Gary Adair

Production
Marcia Deboy
Michael Dietsch
Jennifer Earhart
Cynthia Fields
Maureen West

About the Authors

Greg Simsic

Photoshop 5 Type Magic is Greg's third Photoshop type effects book. Greg has traveled the world designing type effects for the rich and poor, young and old, beautiful and ugly alike. He is driven by the belief that everyone should have some "magic" in their lives even if they don't really deserve it. Despite his busy schedule, he always makes time to come home and spend quality time with his pet yak, Camille. "She grounds me," says Greg. Those who were lucky enough to attend the 65th annual Pixies, the Oscars of the flaming logo world, will keep close to their hearts his overheard words, "I dunno, blur it some."

Acknowledgements

Special Thanks to...

I would like to thank all of the little people for making me seem taller.

I would also like to thank Beth, Kevin, Adam, Kate and all others who transformed my meanders into a book. Those of you who also fit into the first category please take a second bow.

v

Contents at a Glance

Contents

Introduction

You might as well face it. Every time Adobe puts out a new version of Photoshop, you will see another *Type Magic* book in the bookstores. But there is good reason to celebrate with a new book this time because Adobe Photoshop 5.0 contains several great new features, including built-in effects such as drop shadows, glows and bevels, editable text layers, aviind a new History palette that allows for multiple undos. These new features make it easier to get to where you're headed—assuming you know where that is. So, I've gone back through some of the old techniques and brought them back in this book—new and improved. Of course, you won't see some of the old effects because the new features are good enough to have made them obsolete. I skipped over these to bring you a whole new batch of never-seen-before-world-premiere-what-will-they-think-of-next-when-would-I-ever-use-that effects. To top it off, the CD-ROM that they told me they would put in the back of this book includes actions that enable you to apply some of the effects in the book at the touch of a button.

Thanks for stopping by, and I hope you enjoy the book.

Greg Simsic

Before You Start

Welcome

Welcome to this third volume of special type techniques for Adobe Photoshop users. More than a how-to manual, this book is a what-to guide. The steps in this book tell you exactly what you need to do in order to create exactly what you want. Flip through the alphabetized thumbtabs to find the type effect you want to create and follow the concise, explanatory steps. If you need a little extra help, flip to the Photoshop Basics section. But, before you jump into the type treatments, let me tell you a little about how this book works. A quick read now will maximize your time later.

System Setup

Most machines now have plenty of power to run Photoshop. With each new Photoshop upgrade, there is an increase in the amount of memory that it takes to run it, but with so many computers equipped for multimedia these days, the basic requirements seem easy to meet. All of the effects in this book were quickly created on a 132Mhz machine with 72 megabytes of RAM and no special graphics acceleration.

When setting up your system, remember that you can never have too much RAM. Adobe recommends 24 to 32MB to run Photoshop. Allocate as much memory to Photoshop as you possibly can to get the most out of your machine.

It is not crucial, but it will help if you have a CD-ROM drive. A number of the effects in this book use files contained on the CD-ROM bundled with this book. (See Appendix B, "What's on the CD-ROM," for information on accessing those files.) However, even if you don't have a CD-ROM drive, you still can perform most of the effects described in the book.

Adobe Photoshop 5.0

All of the techniques in this book were created with Adobe Photoshop 5.0, and that's the version I recommend you use. If you're attempting to duplicate these techniques using an earlier version of Photoshop, your results might differ slightly or significantly compared to mine. If you work with version 4.0, the biggest deficiency you face is the lack of the new Layer Effects features. I used these features in the book when they made things easier. If you know your way around Photoshop, you can work around most of these situations. Almost all the effects can be created by version 3.0 also, but again beware of the missing Layer Effects. In short, if you have an older version of Photoshop, you can use the techniques in this book as guidelines, but you might not be able to follow them verbatim. Most of the effects in this book use features that were not available in versions of Photoshop earlier than 3.0.

What's New in Adobe Photoshop 5.0

The latest version of Photoshop has many new changes. Some are minor and some are major. Two major new features change the way that you work through these techniques: Layer effects and the History palette. The History palette is Photoshop's name for multiple undos. With the History palette, you can move backward and forward through up to your last 100 steps. Each of the steps appears on the History palette in the order that you performed them. This feature is invaluable when you work through step-by-step techniques such as those provided in this book. To return to a previous stage in the technique, all you have to do is click on the name of the command in the History palette. Or press (Command-Option-Z) [Control-Alt-Z] to move backward through the steps. To move forward again, press (Command-Shift-Z) [Control-Shift-Z].

Layer effects are features that enable you to apply built-in special effects to individual layers. Drop shadows, glows, and bevels are all covered by the layer effects. The interface for these effects is well-designed, making some of the techniques from my previous books obsolete. You can apply more than one effect to a single layer and even apply them to special type layers, also new to Photoshop 5.0, and still have editable text. It is important to remember that these effects are only applied to the layers. The information in the layer has not changed; the effects can be turned on and off at any time. These effects have been used in this book to save time and effort.

Conventions

Almost all the type effects in this book were created as RGB files. Many techniques in this book use filters that will not work in CMYK or Grayscale mode files. You can make your effects in any appropriate color mode, but you should be aware of the differences in the color ranges of the various color modes. Some colors that look great in RGB mode might look like mud after you convert the file color mode to CMYK. If you intend to print your files, it is a good rule to work in the RGB mode (in order to take advantage of all Photoshop's features) and turn on the CMYK preview (in order to keep track of what the colors will look like when turn into a CMYK image). To turn on the CMYK preview, choose View➡CMYK Preview.

If you want more detailed information about the different color modes, refer to a good general Photoshop book such as *Inside Adobe Photoshop 5* or to your Photoshop user manuals.

The type images were also created as 5-inch-by-2-inch, 150dpi resolution files. If you are going to work in a resolution other than 150dpi, remember that some of the filters and commands require different settings than the settings I used. Because a 72dpi image has few pixels, a Gaussian Blur radius of 5 pixels blurs the image more than if it were a 150dpi image. Just keep an eye on the figures next to the steps and match the outcome as close as you can.

The Toolbox

For some of the effects, I used specially prepared preset files. Any of these extras files not included with the standard Photoshop software are listed in the Toolbox in the lower-left corner of the first page of each technique. The Toolbox lists everything that you need to create each type effect and any of its variations. The CD-ROM that comes with this book contains all the files needed to perform all the basic techniques. For information on accessing these files, turn to Appendix B, "What's on the CD-ROM."

The Blue Type

As you work through the steps, you see phrases colored a light blue. These same phrases appear in alphabetical order in the Photoshop Basics section. If the phrase in blue asks you to perform a task that you are unfamiliar with, you can find that phrase in the Photoshop Basics section and follow the instructions on how to perform that task. Advanced users can perform the task as they normally would.

Menu Commands

You also will see instructions that look like this:

Filter➡Blur➡Gaussian Blur (2 pixels)

This example asks you to apply the Gaussian Blur filter. To perform this command, click on the Filter menu at the top of the screen and drag down to Blur. When Blur appears highlighted, a new menu opens to the right, from which you can choose Gaussian Blur.

In this example, a dialog box appears asking you for more information. All the settings that you need to perform each task appear in the text of the step. The preceding example tells you to enter 2 pixels as the Radius.

Click OK to blur the type.

Settings

Following each action in the steps, you will find the settings for that feature. These recommended settings are meant to act as guides; the best settings for your type effect might vary. As a rule of thumb, it is best to match the outcomes that you see in the figures as you progress through the technique. The greatest differences occur when the resolution of your file and/or the point-size of your type are significantly different from what I used. The following two images demonstrate the importance of adjusting for resolution differences. A 6-pixel radius Gaussian Blur was applied to both images.

75 dpi— 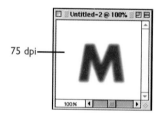 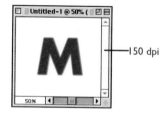 —150 dpi

Tips

Throughout the book, you will find additional bits of information that can help you render a better type effect. These tips provide information beyond the basic steps of each technique. ●

Photoshop Basics

The goal of this section is to help new and novice users of Photoshop with the basic tasks required to create the type effects illustrated in this book. Each of the basic tasks in this section corresponds to the blue highlighted text in the chapters that follow. Here you can easily find the instructions you need for performing a particular Photoshop task.

This chapter proceeds on two assumptions: that you create our type effects in Photoshop 5.0, and that you keep the Tool and Layer/Channel/Path palettes open. If one or both of the Tool and Layer/Channel/Path palettes are closed when you refer to this chapter, you can reopen them by name by using the Window menu at the top of the screen. If you use an earlier version of Photoshop, you can refer to the Photoshop manual for instructions on how to perform these tasks. Keep in mind that these instructions are for Photoshop 5.0 and instructions for earlier versions might differ.

The Toolbox

If you're not familiar with Photoshop's Toolbox, don't panic. With a bit of experimentation, it doesn't take long to learn each tool's individual functions. To help the beginning Photoshop user along the way, here is a representation of the Toolbox. This also helps advanced users find the rearranged tools.

Photoshop 5 Type Magic

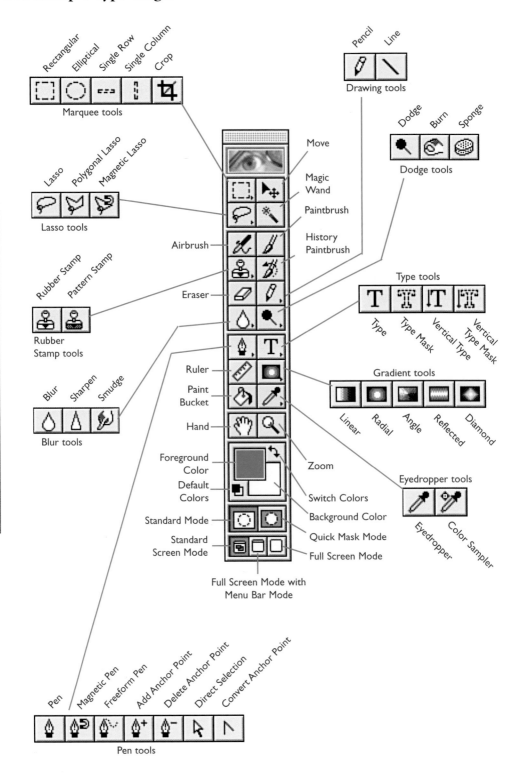

Rectangular · Elliptical · Single Row · Single Column · Crop

Marquee tools

Lasso · Polygonal Lasso · Magnetic Lasso

Lasso tools

Rubber Stamp · Pattern Stamp

Rubber Stamp tools

Blur · Sharpen · Smudge

Blur tools

Pencil · Line

Drawing tools

Dodge · Burn · Sponge

Dodge tools

Move
Magic Wand
Paintbrush
Airbrush
History Paintbrush
Eraser

Type tools

Type · Type Mask · Vertical Type · Vertical Type Mask

Ruler
Paint Bucket
Hand

Gradient tools

Linear · Radial · Angle · Reflected · Diamond

Foreground Color
Default Colors
Zoom

Eyedropper tools

Switch Colors
Background Color

Eyedropper · Color Sampler

Standard Mode
Standard Screen Mode
Quick Mask Mode
Full Screen Mode

Full Screen Mode with Menu Bar Mode

Pen · Magnetic Pen · Freeform Pen · Add Anchor Point · Delete Anchor Point · Direct Selection · Convert Anchor Point

Pen tools

6

Basic Photoshop Tasks

Choose a Foreground or Background Color

Shortcuts: Press D to change colors to their defaults: black for the foreground and white for the background.

Press X to switch the foreground color with the background color.

You can choose a foreground color from two palettes. Choose a foreground color from the Swatch palette by clicking on one of the swatches. To choose a background color from the Swatches palette, hold the (Option) [Alt] key while clicking on the swatch. Or choose a color from the Color palette by either using the sliders or entering numeric values. To enter the values using a specific color model such as CMYK, choose that model from the Color palette menu.

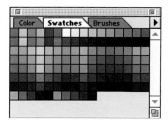
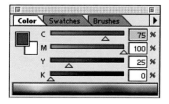

Foreground color — Switch colors (X)
Default Colors (D) — Background color

To choose a foreground or background color, click on either the Foreground color icon or the Background color icon on the Toolbox.

The Color Picker dialog box appears offering two methods for choosing a color. To change the color that appears in the large area on the left, use the sliders on either side of the vertical spectrum. To select a color, click in the area on the left. You can also choose a color by entering numeric values. All of the colors I used in these techniques have been specified by their CMYK values. Enter these values as percentages in the appropriate input boxes in the lower right. Note that the Foreground and Background icons on the Toolbox now reflect your color choices.

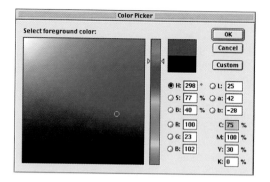

Create a New Channel

Shortcuts: Click the New Channel icon on the Channels palette. Hold the (Option) [Alt] key while clicking the New Channel icon to create a new channel and open the New Channel dialog box.

To create a new channel, choose New Channel from the Channels palette pop-up menu.

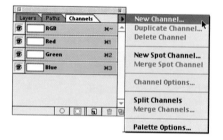

Use the New Channel dialog box to establish your settings. Unless noted otherwise, I used the default settings when creating a new channel. This figure shows Photoshop's default settings.

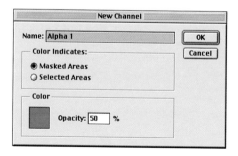

8

Create a New File

Shortcuts: Press (Command-N) [Control-N].

To create a new file, choose File➡New. The New dialog box appears, which is where you name your new file and establish other settings. Almost all images in this book were begun by creating a file with these settings: Width: 5 inches, Height: 2 inches, Resolution: 150 pixels/inch, Mode: RGB Color, Contents: White.

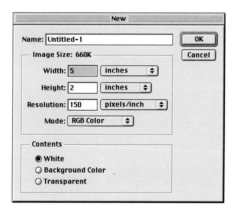

Create a New Layer

Shortcuts: Click the New Layer icon on the Layers palette. Hold the (Option) [Alt] key while clicking the New Layer icon to create a new layer and open the New Layer dialog box.

To create a new layer, choose New Layer from the Layer palette pop-up menu, or choose Layer➡New➡Layer. Or you can press (Command-Shift-N) [Control-Shift-N].

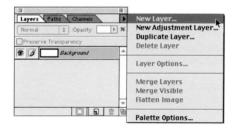

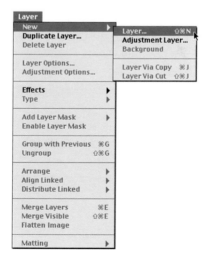

9

The New Layer dialog box opens, which is where you name the new layer and establish other settings.

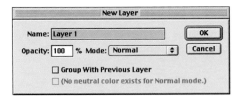

Delete a Channel

To delete a channel, select the channel on the Channels palette and click on the Trash icon at the bottom of the palette. You can also drag it to the Trash icon (just like you would to get rid of a document on the Desktop by dragging it to the Trash or the Recycle Bin). Finally, you also can select the channel and choose Delete Channel from the Channels palette menu.

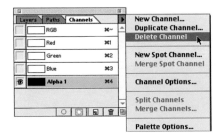

Delete a Layer

To delete a layer, select the layer on the Layers palette and click on the Trash icon at the bottom of the palette. You can also drag it to the Trash icon (just like you would to get rid of a document on the Desktop by dragging it to the Trash). Finally, you also can select the layer and choose Delete Layer from the Layers palette menu.

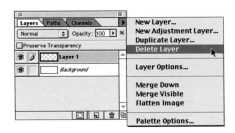

10

Deselect the Selection
Shortcut: Press (Command-D) [Control-D].

To deselect a selection, choose Select➡Deselect. The marquee disappears. If you have accidentally deselected a selection, you can choose Select➡Reselect to bring back the last active selection.

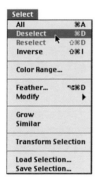

Duplicate a Channel
Shortcut: On the Channels palette, select the channel you want to duplicate and drag it on top of the New Channel icon. Hold the (Option) [Alt] key while dragging the channel to the New Channel icon to create a new channel and open the Duplicate Channel dialog box.

To create a duplicate of a channel, make the channel active and then select Duplicate Channel from the Channels palette menu.

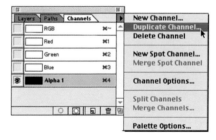

A new copy of the channel you selected for duplication is created automatically, and the Duplicate Channel dialog box appears.

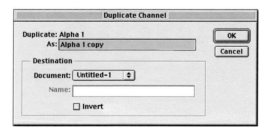

Enter the Text

Photoshop 5.0 has four type tools. There is a standard Type tool and a Type Mask tool, and each of these tools has a counterpart tool that allows them to place type in vertical columns. In this book, I used only the standard Type tool and the Type Mask tool. Each effect in this book specifies which type tool to use.

The standard Type tool enters the type into a new layer. The color of the type defaults to the foreground color, but you can also select the color by clicking on the color swatch in the Type dialog box. This new layer is marked in the Layers palette by a "T" next to the layer preview on the Layers palette. If you want to edit the text, double-click the "T" to reopen the Type dialog box. These editable type layers can have layer effects (accessible from the Layers menu) applied to them and you can use the Transform tools on them, but you cannot use all of Photoshop's features to manipulate these layers. In order to do so, you must render the layer by choosing Layer➡Type➡Render Layer. After you apply this command, the "T" disappears from the Layers palette and you can no longer edit the type. The instructions direct you to apply this command when necessary.

The Type Mask tool creates selection outlines of the text you enter without filling the outlines with a color, and without creating a new layer.

In some effects, the instructions in this book ask you to enter text into a channel. Unless noted otherwise, it is assumed that you are entering white text onto the black background of the channel.

To enter the text, select the type tool specified in the instructions, and then click any-where in the image to open the Type Tool dialog box. Type the text in the large box at the bottom of the dialog box, and make your attribute choices from the preceding options. Because many of the effects in this book apply effects that spread the type, you might find it desirable to increase the spacing between the letters of the words. To do this, enter a positive amount in the Tracking input box. Unless noted otherwise in the instructions, always make sure that you have the Anti-Aliased box checked.

12

After clicking OK, move the type into position with the Move (standard Type tool) or Marquee (Type Mask tool) tool.

Fill

In this book, fill normally means to fill the selection with a color. To fill a selection with the foreground color, press (Option-Delete) [Alt-Delete]. To fill the selection with the background color, press (Command-Delete) [Control-Delete]. If you are in the Background layer or any layer that has the Preserve Transparency option turned on, you can press Delete to fill in the selection with the Background color.

You also can fill a selection by choosing Edit➡Fill or pressing Shift-Delete.

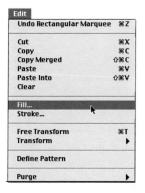

The Fill dialog box opens, allowing you several fill Contents choices as well as the ability to set the Blending Opacity and Mode.

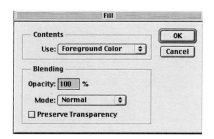

If the Preserve Transparency option is turned on for a layer, using any fill method only fills the areas of that layer already filled—transparent areas remain transparent. If a selection is empty (contains a transparent area of a layer) and the Preserve Transparency option is turned on for that layer, then you cannot fill the selection. To fill the selection, simply turn off the Preserve Transparency option before filling it.

Group/Ungroup a Layer

Shortcut: Select the layer on top and press (Command-G) [Control-G] to group it with the layer below. Press Shift and (Command-G) [Control-G] to ungroup it.

13

To group one layer with another, hold the (Option) [Alt] key and click on the line that divides the two layers. Or select the layer on top and choose Layer➡Group with Previous. The solid line between the layers will be replaced with a dotted line. To ungroup the layers, (Option) [Alt] click on the dotted line, or choose Layer➡Ungroup.

Intersect the Selection

Shortcut: Hold down the Shift and (Option) [Alt] keys and click on the channel or layer that contains the selection to be intersected with the current selection.

Intersecting one selection with another selection results in a new selection that contains only areas that were part of both of the original selections. To do this, one selection needs to be active. Then either perform the previous shortcut or choose Select➡Load Selection to open the Load Selection dialog box. Choose the channel as the source and turn on the Intersect with Selection operation at the bottom. If you click on a layer as described in the shortcut method, the current selection intersects with the layer's transparency selection.

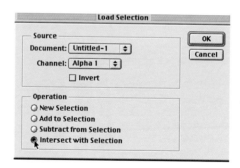

Link/Unlink a Layer

To link one layer with another, make one of the layers active and click in the box that is just to the left of the other layer's preview. A small chain link icon appears in the box. To unlink the layer, click on the Chain Link icon.

14

Load a Selection

Shortcut: Hold down the (Command) [Control] key and click on the channel (on the Channels palette) that contains the selection you want to load. Or hold down (Command) [Control] and type the number of the channels whose selection you want to load.

To load a selection, choose Select➡Load Selection. This opens the Load Selection dialog box where you can establish document, channel, and operation variables.

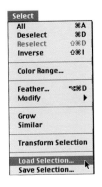

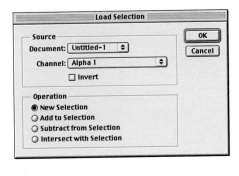

Load the Transparency Selection (of a Layer)

To load the transparency selection of a layer, hold down the (Command) [Control] key and click on the layer (on the Layers palette) that contains the transparency selection you want to load. The selection encompasses all nontransparent areas of that layer.

15

Make a Channel Active

To make a channel active for editing or modification, click on its thumbnail or name on the Channels palette. If you make the RGB channel (referred to as the composite channel in this book) active, all the color channels (Red, Green, and Blue) become active.

Photoshop 5 Type Magic

You can tell the channel is active if it is highlighted with a color.

Make a Channel Visible/Invisible

If you see an eye in the left-most column next to a channel, that channel is visible. To make a channel visible, click in that column to turn on the Eye icon. Click on the eye to remove it and make the channel invisible. If you make the RGB channel (referred to as the composite channel in this book) visible or invisible, all the color channels (Red, Green, and Blue) become visible or invisible.

Make a Layer Active

To make a layer active, click on its thumbnail or title in the Layers palette.

You can tell the layer is active if it is highlighted with a color.

Make a Layer Visible/Invisible

If you see an eye in the left-most column next to a layer, that layer is visible. To make a layer visible, click in that column to turn on the Eye icon. Click on the eye to remove it and make the layer invisible.

Move a Layer

To move a Layer, click on the layer you want to move in the Layers palette and drag it up or down the list of layers to the place you want to move it. As you drag the layer, the lines between the layers darken to indicate where the layer will fall if you let go. You can also use the keyboard to move layers. Press (Command-Option-]) [Control-Alt-]] to move the layer up one layer. Press (Command-Option-[) [Control-Alt-[] to move the layer down one layer.

The layer you moved appears between layers, numerically "out of order."

Return to the Composite Channel

Shortcut: Press (Command-~) [Control-~].

If you want to return to the composite channel, click on its thumbnail or title (RGB, CMYK, Lab). The composite channel is always the one with (Command-~) [Control-~] after its title.

Photoshop 5 Type Magic

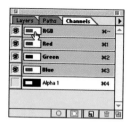

If you are in an RGB file, channels 0 through 3 are now active because each of the R, G, and B channels are individual parts of the RGB channel.

Save a File

Shortcut: Press (Command-Shift-S) [Control-Shift-S] to save a file with a new name, or press (Command-S) [Control-S] to save changes to the current file.

To save a file with a new name, choose File➡Save As. The Save As dialog box opens, in which you can name your new file and choose a format. To save changes to the current file, choose File➡Save.

File format selection depends on what you have in your file, what you want to keep when you save it, and what you're going to do with the file after it is saved. Consult a detailed Photoshop book, such as *Inside Adobe Photoshop 5*, for more guidance on which file format is best for your needs.

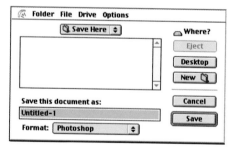

Save a Selection

Shortcut: Click the Save Selection icon on the Channels palette.

To save a selection, choose Select➡Save Selection.

The Save Selection dialog box opens. Choose your options and click OK to save the selection.

Subtract from the Selection

Shortcut: Hold down the (Option) [Alt] key and click on the channel or layer that contains the selection to be subtracted from the current selection.

Subtracting one selection from another selection results in a new selection that contains all areas of the original selection that are not part of the second selection. To do this, first make a selection. Then either perform the previous shortcut or choose Select➡Load Selection to open the Load Selection dialog box. Choose the channel as the source and turn on the Subtract from Selection operation at the bottom. If you click on a layer as described in the shortcut method, the layer's transparency selection will be subtracted from the current selection.

19

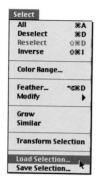

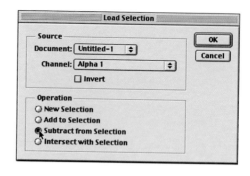

Turn on/off Preserve Transparency

To turn on or off the Preserve Transparency option for a particular layer, first make that layer the active layer. Then click the Preserve Transparency check box on the Layers palette. This option is not available for the Background layer. ●

This effect demonstrates several methods for manipulating stock images that can be pasted together to form words. Each new word that you "assemble" requires its own unique solutions, but this example presents some useful techniques.

1 Create a new file, and use the Type tool to enter the text (Helvetica Bold at 100 points). This type layer will be used as a guide when pasting together the various images. Use a simple sans serif typeface such as Helvetica. It is also wise to enter a positive Tracking value (I used +50) in order to spread the letters apart.

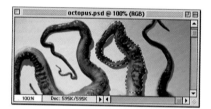

2 Next open a file that contains an image to be used as a part of one of the letters. One of the tentacles in this octopus image (Octopus.psd from PhotoDisc) forms a perfect "P." All five images used for this effect came from PhotoDisc files on the P5TM CD (P5TM➡Images➡ PhotoDisc).

3 Use the selection tools to select the part of the image you want to use, copy it, and close the file. Paste the image into the file containing the type.

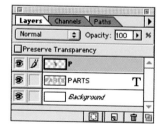

4 Each time you use the Paste command, the image is conveniently placed onto a new layer. This is very helpful in keeping all of the letters and images organized. After the new layer is created, double-click on the layer name and change the name of the layer to the letter that it will contain.

5 Use the Move tool to shift the piece into place. The tentacle needs to be flipped. Choose Edit➡ Transform➡Flip Horizontal. Then press (Command-T) [Control-T] so that you can use the Transform handles to shape the image and rotate it slightly counterclockwise. The tentacle needs to be scaled to fit the size of the letters in the guide. Press (Return) [Enter] to accept the changes.

6 For the "A," copy this coat hanger from another PhotoDisc image (OS05021.TIF) and cut off the metal hook. Paste it into the image file; press (Command-T) [Control-T] and use the Transform handles to squeeze the ends together and stretch its height slightly.

7 Press (Return) [Enter] to accept the changes and then use the Lasso tool to select the crossbar only. Choose Layer➡New➡Layer Via Cut. Move the new layer (renamed "A2") below the original "A" layer and use the Move tool to shift it into place.

 TIP

If you want to blend two parts of a letter together, merge those two layers by making the top layer active and choose Merge Down from the Layers palette. Then use the Smudge tool to blur the images together.

23

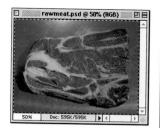

8 I used a different strategy to make the "R." I opened a file that contained an image of a piece of raw beef (rawmeat.psd from PhotoDisc), chose Select➡All, copied it, and closed the file.

9 Use the Type Mask tool to enter the letter "R." Then choose Edit➡Paste Into to paste the raw meat image into the type selection. A layer mask is created for this layer. Drag the layer mask to the trash icon at the bottom of the Layers palette and click "Apply" in the dialog box that asks if you want to do so.

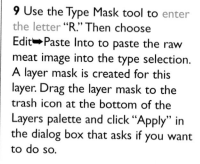

10 To give the meat a little dimension, choose Layer➡Effects➡Bevel and Emboss. Choose the Inner Bevel style, raise the Depth to 15 pixels, and raise the Blur amount enough so that the letter appears rounded (15 pixels).

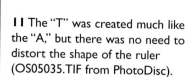

11 The "T" was created much like the "A," but there was no need to distort the shape of the ruler (OS05035.TIF from PhotoDisc).

12 I copied this pipe from the OS05041.TIF PhotoDisc image and pasted it into a new layer over the "S." Use the Free Transform command again (Command-T) [Control-T] to scale and rotate the pipe. I also chose Edit➧ Transform➧ Flip Horizontal to flip the image.

13 Press (Return) [Enter] to accept the changes; select the Rectangular Marquee tool and select a rectangle around the pipe. The Shear filter used in the next step distorts the pipe within the boundaries set by the marquee selection.

14 Choose Filter➧Distort➧Shear to open the Shear dialog box. This filter is great at getting curves out of linear shapes. Click and drag points on the graph to shape the pipe.

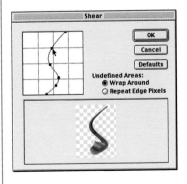

TIP The filters in the Filter➧Distort submenu are the most useful filters for manipulating the shapes of images into the letters. Try Pinch, Spherize, Shear, Twirl, Polar Coordinates, and Wave.

15 Press (Command-T) [Control-T] again and hold the (Command) [Control] key while dragging the top-right corner in toward the center of the pipe. Use the Transform handles to make any other changes and press (Return) [Enter] to accept the changes.

16 Here's what I have so far.

And here is what the Layers palette looks like.

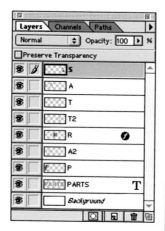

17 Use the Drop Shadow feature to apply a shadow to one layer and then choose Layer➡Effects➡Copy Effects. Link all of the other layers (by clicking in the box to the right of the eye on the Layers palette) that contain the letters and choose Layer➡Effects➡Paste Effects to Linked to apply the Drop Shadow to all layers. The shadow looks great on letters such as the "A" and "T" in which one part overlaps another.

18 Delete the original type layer to let the images stand on their own. After seeing the type without the type guide behind it, you may want make adjustments. I used the Transform feature once again to increase the size of the "R" and to rotate it back a little.   ●

Follow the bouncing balls, or rather the numbered steps, to create a shaded sphere onto which you can lay type. This effect relies on a custom gradient for the Radial Gradient tool and the new 3D Transform filter that seems custom made for laying the type onto the balls.

1 Create a new file and create a new layer (Layer 1). Click and hold the pointer on the Marquee tool. Scroll through the different Marquee tools and select the Elliptical Marquee tool.

2 With the Elliptical Marquee tool, draw a circle. If you hold down the Shift key while dragging, the selection will be constrained to a perfect circle.

3 Change the foreground color to a color for the ball, and change the background color to the color for the shadow. For the ball, I used a yellow (CMYK: 4, 1, 51, 0), and for the shadow, I used black (CMYK: 60, 60, 60, 100).

4 Double-click the Radial Gradient tool to select it and to display the Radial Gradient Options palette. Choose Foreground to Background from the Gradient pop-up menu.

5 Click the Edit button on the Radial Gradient Options palette. A new dialog box appears. Click the tab in the lower left that has an "F" inside it. "F" stands for foreground color. Then click just below the colored gradient. The color at the location of the pointer is the foreground color. Drag the new "F" marker until the Location field reads 22%.

6 Grab the diamond above the colored gradient that is to the right of the marker you just placed. Drag it to the right until the Location field reads 62%. Click OK to save your changes to the Foreground to Background gradient.

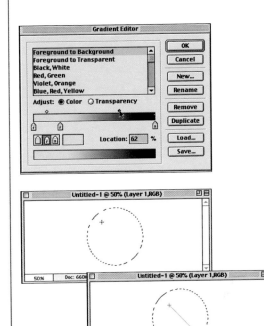

7 Now, back to the circle selection. Click and drag the Radial Gradient tool from the upper-left part of the active selection to the lower-right part of the selection as shown here.

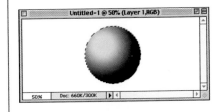

Here's what I got. If you don't like what you get, press (Command-Z) [Control-Z] and repeat this step.

29

8 Change the foreground color to a color for the type. I used black. Then use the Type tool to enter the text for the ball. I used 80-point Matrix Bold. The type drops automatically into a new layer. Use the Move tool to position the type in the center of the sphere, and choose Layer➡Type➡Render Layer.

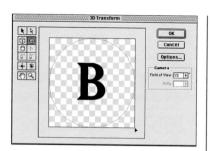

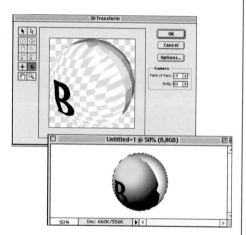

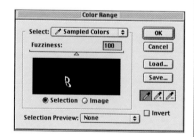

9 Load the transparency selection of Layer 1, but keep the type layer the active layer. Choose Filter➡Render➡3D Transform. This dialog box has its own set of tools. Select the Sphere tool. Then click the pointer on the upper-left corner of the preview box. Then drag the pointer to the right on top of the bottom-right corner of the preview. This creates a sphere that is the same size as the selection you made in Step 2. (Note: The sphere looks like a circle until you rotate it in the next step.)

10 Select the Trackball tool on the Tool palette (highlighted in the figure). Then click the pointer inside the circle and drag it to rotate the sphere and type. Use this tool to position the type as you want.

TIP If, as you rotate the sphere, part of the sphere moves out of the preview window, use the Pan Camera tool to center it again inside the preview window. The Pan Camera tool is the tool to the left of the Trackball tool.

11 Click OK and deselect the selection. This filter renders some undesirable grayscale shading on the backside of the sphere that has peeked around at the edge. The foreground color should still be the same as the color of the type. Make sure that it is, make Layer 1 invisible, and choose Select➡Color Range. The type will automatically be selected. Set the Fuzziness so that only the type is selected (100).

Click OK and choose Select➡
Inverse. Press Delete to get rid of
the shading. Deselect the selection.

> **If deleting the Color Range
> selection gets rid of some
> of your type, press
> (Command-Z) [Control-Z]
> to undo the Delete com-
> mand.** Deselect the selec-
> tion **and use the Lasso tool
> to draw a new selection
> around the type. Then do
> Step 11 to delete the shad-
> ing.**

12 Make Layer 1 visible again to
see the final image.

VARIATIONS

Highlight

Change the Foreground color to white. Double-click the Radial Gradient tool and use the settings that you see here.

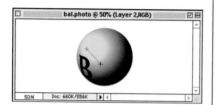

Create a new layer (Layer 2), and drag the Radial Gradient tool from the center of the highlight outward just a short distance.

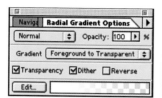

Here is the highlight.

Glossy

To make glossier balls, perform previous Steps 1 through 3, except in Step 3, choose white for the foreground color and black for the background color. You can do this by pressing D and then X. The circle selection should still be active. Perform Steps 4 through 7.

Then make a new layer and name it Color. Keep the selection active. Choose a foreground color for the color of the ball, and fill the selection. The gradation disappears. From the pop-up menu on the Layers palette, change the layer blending mode to Color. There is your shiny ball. Complete Steps 8 through 12 to add the text.

Billiard Balls

To turn that ball into a billiard ball, use preceding the Glossy method. After finishing Step 7, create a new layer and select the Elliptical Marquee tool again. Deselect the selection. Then click and drag a perfect circle on top of the ball. Change the foreground color to white and fill the selection.

After Step 8, choose Merge Down from the Layers palette menu to merge the type layer with the white circle. Perform Steps 8 through 10. You probably cannot use Color Range in Step 11. You'd be better off to use the Lasso tool to select and delete the shading. Here is how the type turned out. ●

33

TOOLBOX

Diamond Brush

Converting a type selection into a path allows you to use the Stroke Paths command to "paint" borders around the edges of the type.

1 Create a new file and create a new layer (Layer 1). Then use the Type Mask tool to enter the text (Triplex Ultra Bold at 110 points). The Stroke Paths command strokes the path right along its center; it affects the areas just inside and just outside of the path. Tight letterspacing can therefore cause problems. Increase the Tracking amount to spread the letters. I set it at 250.

2 Find the Paths palette and choose Make Work Path (Tolerance: 1 pixel) from the Paths palette menu to turn the selection into a path.

3 Select the Paintbrush tool. The Stroke Subpaths command used in Step 7 can stroke the path with a variety of tools. The default tool is the currently selected tool (as long as that tool is one of the possible options). This list displays all the tools that the Stroke Paths command can use.

4 Find the Brushes palette and choose Load Brushes from the Brushes palette menu. On the P5TM CD-ROM find the Diamond Brush file (P5TM➡P5TM Files➡Brushes➡Diamond Brush). You can create borders with any brush. For this effect, I created this diamond brush. Select the diamond brush added at the bottom of the Brushes palette.

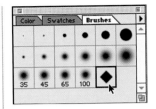

5 Choose a foreground color for the diamond. (I used CMYK: 72, 0, 72, 0.) The Stroke Paths command pushes the Paintbrush along the path using the diamond brush and "paints" with the foreground color.

6 Double-click on the diamond brush to open the Brush Options dialog box. Set the Spacing to 100%. As the Stroke Path command push-es the brush along the path, it uses this Spacing percentage to deter-mine how far it moves before plac-ing another diamond.

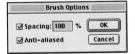

7 Click on the Stroke Path icon on the bottom of the Paths palette or choose Stroke Path from the Paths palette menu.

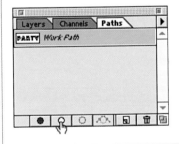

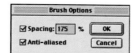

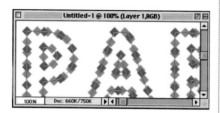

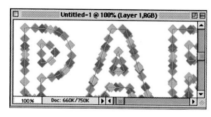

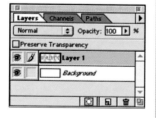

8 Choose another foreground color (CMYK: 100, 50, 0, 0) and then double-click on the diamond brush again. Set the Spacing to 175%.

9 Click on the Stroke Path icon again.

10 Repeat Steps 8 and 9 using a new color (CMYK: 50, 0, 0, 0) and a new brush spacing (250%).

11 Create a new layer (Layer 2) and change the layer blending mode to Difference. Then Repeat Steps 8 and 9 again (CMYK: 0, 75, 100, 0; Brush Spacing: 150%). Changing the blending mode to Difference produces new colors in the diamonds by partially inverting some of the colors in Layer 1. The diamonds look like they intersect rather than just overlap.

12 Choose Turn Off Path from the Paths palette menu and Merge Down from the Layers palette menu.

36

13 Then choose Filter➡
Distort➡Ripple (Amount: 200%,
Size: Medium). Finish the type off
with a drop shadow. Adjust the
Amount as necessary to distort the
diamonds without obliterating
them.

Designing Borders

You might think that by stroking
the path more than once and using
different brushes and colors you
can create patterns to run along
the borders of type. But this is diffi-
cult, if not impossible, because it is
hard to match the spacing of different size and shape brushes.
However, you can use one closely
spaced brush to create a background texture and then use another sparsely spaced brush to run an
image on top of the border.

1 Do previous Steps 1 through 3.
Then in Step 4, load the Assorted
Brushes file included in Photoshop
5.0 (Adobe Photoshop➡Goodies➡
Brushes & Patterns➡Assorted
Brushes). A variety of new brushes
appear in the Brushes palette.
Select the large star brush shown
here.

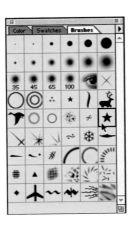

2 Here is the foreground color I
used in Step 5: CMYK: 100, 50, 0,
40. I left the Brush Spacing at the
default (25%) in Step 6. Do Step 7
to stroke the path.

37

STARS

3 Double-click on the smaller star brush to select it and open the Brush Options dialog box. Set the Spacing to 100%. Choose a new foreground color (CMYK: 0, 0, 100, 0) and click on the Stroke Path icon again.

Masks

1 Open a file containing the image that you want to mask. I opened an image provided in the Photoshop 5.0 Samples folder (Adobe Photoshop 5.0➧Sample➧Big sky). Copy the image and close the file. Create a new file and paste in the image. It will be placed into a new layer (Layer 1).

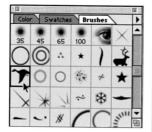

2 Then choose Layer➧Add Layer Mask➧Hide All. The image disappears. The layer mask becomes the active channel. Select the Paintbrush tool and choose white for the foreground color. Double-click on this Duck brush to open the Brush Options dialog box. Set the Spacing at 75%.

3 Use the Type Mask tool to enter the text (Triplex Ultra Bold at 140 points, Tracking: 250) and then choose Make Work Path from the Paths palette menu (Tolerance: 1 pixel).

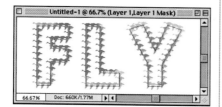

4 Select the Paintbrush tool and click on the Stroke Path icon on the Paths palette. The image is revealed beneath the ducks.

5 Finally, I add an Inner Bevel and a Drop Shadow to Layer 1.

VARIATIONS

Something Simple

After creating a border for the type with a simple round brush (Spacing: 100%), I used the Inner Bevel layer effect to make the circles look like balls. A drop shadow finished the image.

Something Not

You can apply other effects in the book to the type borders. I used the same round brush to create a border and then used the Chrome effect on page 50 to make this image. ●

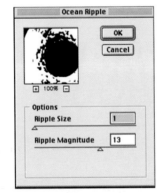

TOOLBOX

Cereal (Lighting
Effects Style)

The unlikely Ocean Ripple filter
works with the Lighting Effects filter to round out these crunchy letters.

1 Create a new file, and a new
channel (Alpha 1). Use the Type
tool to enter the text. Font choice
for this effect is important. I used
Thickhead (110 points) because the
shapes of the letters look like bul-
bous Cheerios.

2 Save the selection to create the
Alpha 2 channel, which will be identical to Alpha 1. Keep the text
selection active.

3 Choose Filter➡Distort➡Ocean
Ripple. This filter distorts the type
around the edges by spreading the
background into the selection. Try
these settings to distort just parts
of the type: Ripple Size: 1; Ripple
Magnitude: 13.

TIP This filter is somewhat
unpredictable, and if the
word you typed is too long,
the Ocean Ripple filter
might distort some of the
letters too much. If this
happens, try selecting only
a few of the letters at a
time and apply the filter.
Continue until the Ocean
Ripple filter has been
applied to all the letters.
Then load the selection
from the Alpha 2 channel
to select all the letters
again.

4 Next, choose Filter➡Blur➡
Gaussian Blur. Blur the text enough
to smooth out the distortion created by the Ocean Ripple filter. I set
the Radius at 8.8.

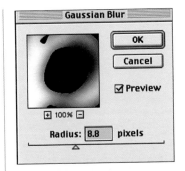

5 Create a new channel (Alpha 3)
and make it the active channel. The
selection should still be active.
Choose Filter➡Pixelate➡
Mezzotint. Select the Coarse Dots
option from the pop-up menu.

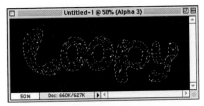

6 Make the Alpha 1 channel active
and then load the Alpha 3 channel
selection.

7 Choose Image➡Adjust➡
Brightness/Contrast. Lower the
Brightness value to about -35. The
dark areas created will aid the
Lighting Effects filter in adding the
pock marks to the surface of the
cereal. Deselect the selection.

41

8 Load the Alpha 2 channel selection. Choose Filter➡Noise➡Add
Noise. Set the Amount to approximately 4 (Distribution: Gaussian).
The noise helps create some shal-
lower bumps in the cereal letters
but keep it low. You will barely see
a change in the image but have
faith. It will make a difference in the
final image.

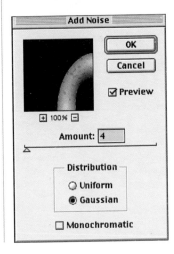

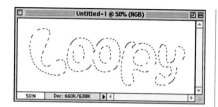

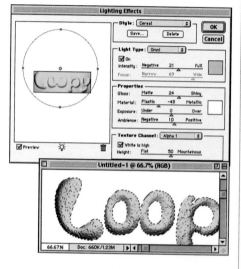

9 Return to the composite channel. Keep the selection active. Make sure that you are in a layer with a flat white background, not a new transparent layer.

10 Choose Filter➡Render➡ Lighting Effects. Choose the Cereal preset from the Style pop-up menu, or match the settings in this figure. Use the Texture Channel Height to adjust the fullness of the letters.

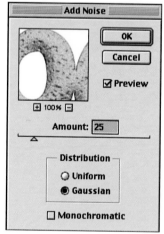

11 As a final touch, I chose Filter➡Noise➡Add Noise and adjusted the Amount to 25. This noise gives the cereal texture a little graininess, and we all know how important grain is to our diets.

VARIATIONS

I just couldn't resist adding this milky background and a shadow.

If you have a hard-edged font that you want to round off for this effect, follow these steps.

In Step 1, use the Type Mask tool instead of the Type tool. This font is Impact at 100 points.

Then choose Select➡Modify➡ Smooth. You might have to try different settings before you get the one you want. I smoothed the selection 10 pixels.

Fill the selection with white and finish the steps preceding (Steps 2 through 11). ●

Making a checkered pattern takes only a few steps. After you learn the steps, you can use Photoshop's filters to make some unique effects including Reflector and Woven type.

1 Create a new file, and create a new layer (Layer 1). Change the foreground color to one of the colors you want to use for the checkers and fill the entire layer with the color. I used the CMYK values 10, 8, 100, and 0.

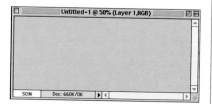

2 Double-click the Marquee tool to select it and to bring the Marquee Options floating palette to the front. Change the style to Fixed Size, and set the Width and Height to 10 pixels. These dimensions determine the size of the squares in the checkered pattern—adjust it to your liking, but make sure you always keep the Width and Height the same.

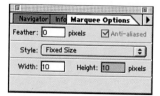

3 Next, click in the image area once with the Marquee tool. A square selection appears. Change the foreground color to the second color for the checkers. I used the CMYK values 90, 60, 30, and 60. Fill the selection with this color.

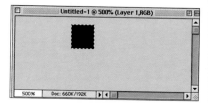

4 Grab the Move tool and hold the (Option) [Alt] key as you drag the selection so that the upper-left corner of the selection meets the lower-right corner of the original colored square. This creates a copy of the original selection in the new position.

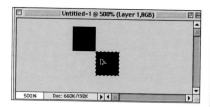

5 Again, select the Marquee tool and find the Marquee Options floating palette. Keep the Style set at Fixed Size and double the Width and Height sizes (20 pixels for me).

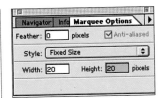

6 Use the Marquee tool to click in the image area. Drag the new, larger, square selection so that it includes both of the colored squares. It should be a perfect match.

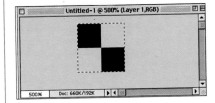

7 Choose Edit➡Define Pattern. There is no dialog box here. Photoshop uses the checks as the pattern for the Fill command used in Step 9. Choose Select➡All, and press Delete to clear the image window. Deselect the selection.

8 Use the Type Mask tool to enter the text. I used Frutiger Ultra Black at 80 points.

9 Choose Edit➡Fill. In the dialog box, change the Contents option to Pattern (Opacity: 100%, Mode: Normal). Click OK, and you have checkers.

Reflector

If you make a few alterations to the steps, you can make a diagonal checkered pattern that I used to make this Reflector effect.

1 Do the previous Steps 1 through 6 to create a four-square pattern. In Step 2, I set the Width and Height to 7 pixels and in Step 5, I used 14 pixels. After completing Step 6, choose Edit➡Transform➡Numeric. Check only the Rotate box and set the angle to 45°. The diamonds will look jagged.

2 Again, find the Marquee Options floating palette. Change the Style to Constrained Aspect Ratio and make sure that the Width and Height settings are changed to 1. This option keeps the selection a perfect square. Drag the Marquee to make a selection like this:

46

3 Do Steps 7 through 9 of the Checkered instructions to define the diagonal pattern, create the type, and fill it with the pattern.

4 Make a new layer (Layer 2). Double-click the Linear Gradient tool to select it and bring to the front the Linear Gradient Options floating palette. Choose the Spectrum preset gradient.

5 Drag the Gradient tool diagonally across the type selection.

The selection fills with the gradient.

6 Change the Layer 2 blending mode to Color. The diamonds reappear.

7 Keep the selection active and make Layer 1 the active layer.

8 Choose Filter➟Render➟ Difference Clouds to complete the effect.

Banana
SEATS-R-US

Woven

1 Do Steps 1 and 2 of the Reflector instructions. (I set the Width and Height to 15 pixels for the first square and 30 pixels to select the four-square pattern.) Then choose Edit➟Define Pattern. Choose Select➟All and Edit➟Fill (Use: Pattern, Opacity: 100%, Mode: Normal) to fill the layer with the diamond pattern. Deselect the selection and choose Flatten Image from the Layers palette menu.

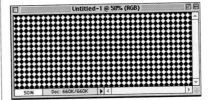

47

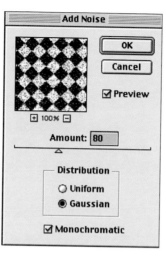

2 Add a little noise to the checks by choosing Filter➡Noise➡Add Noise. I set the Amount to 80 (Gaussian). Turn on the Monochromatic option. The noise helps the next filter do its job.

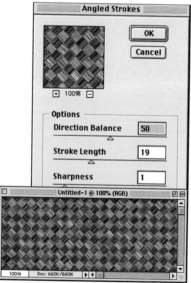

3 Apply Filter➡Brush Strokes➡Angled Strokes. Use these settings: Direction Balance, 50; Stroke Length, 19; and Sharpness, 1. Adjust the settings if necessary. You want to see some good streaks through the checks, but be careful not to obliterate them.

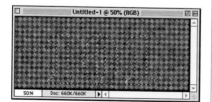

4 Now, we need some type. Use the Type Mask tool to enter the text. This font is Seagull Heavy at 135 points.

5 Choose Select➡Inverse, make sure the foreground color is white, and press Option-Delete. Then choose Select➡Inverse again to select the type.

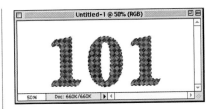

6 And we need some color. Choose Image➡Adjust➡ Hue/Saturation. Now turn on the Colorize option and find a color for the texture.

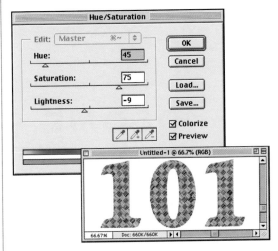

7 For some fine-tuning, choose Image➡Adjust➡Levels. Use the Input markers to adjust the values in the weave. I set the Input markers at 21, 0.88, and 255. For a darker, more contrasty pattern, click the Auto button. ●

Following are three methods for creating shiny metallic type. The first combines Photoshop 5.0's Inner Bevel layer effect with some "magic" Curves. The second uses a channel and the Lighting Effects filter and the third is an airbrushed chrome look that uses the Gradient tool.

Layer Effects Chrome

1 Create a new file, choose 50% gray for the foreground color, and use the Type tool to enter the text. (I used Copperplate Gothic Thirty Three BC at 95 points.) This technique works better with thin typefaces. Don't use anything too heavy and blocky. Choose Layer➡Type➡ Render Layer.

2 Choose Layer➡Effects➡Bevel and Emboss. Select the Inner Bevel style, raise the Depth to 20 pixels, and then raise the Blur amount until the type looks rounded (15 pixels).

TOOLBOX

Chrome Curves, Chrome (Lighting Effects Style)

3 Choose Layer➥Effects➥Create Layers. Two layers will be added to the Layers palette—one for the bevel highlights and one for the shadows. From the Layers palette menu, choose Merge Group. The two new layers will be merged back into the original layer.

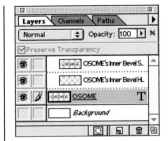

4 Choose Image➥Adjust➥ Curves, click the Load button, and find the Chrome Curves file on the P5TM CD-ROM (P5TM➥P5TM Files➥Curves➥ Chrome Curves).

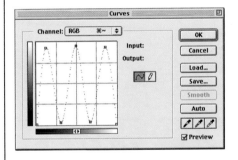

Click OK to get something like this.

5 Choose Image➡Adjust➡Curves again. The Curves dialog box is an excellent tool for adding some subtle color to the type. From the menu at the top, select only one of the color channels. (I used Blue.) Grab the line on the graph in the center and bend toward the upper-left corner to add a blue tint to the type and bend it toward the lower-right corner to make a warmer chrome. Selecting and adjusting other color channels will result in different effects.

6 A drop shadow finishes off the effect and brings out the lighter colors in the lower-right parts of the letters.

Color Variations

For more drastic color changes, choose Image➡Adjust➡Hue/Saturation and use all three sliders to change the color. Here are two examples.

Lighting Effects Chrome

1 Create a new file and create a new channel (Alpha 1). Use the Type Mask tool to enter the text (OCR-B at 85 points). Save the selection to create the Alpha 2 channel.

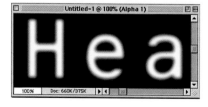

2 Fill the text selection with white and deselect the selection. Choose Filter➡Blur➡Gaussian Blur (3.5 pixels).

3 Load the selection of the active channel and choose Filter➡Blur➡Gaussian Blur. Set the Radius to at least twice as high as in the last step (9 pixels).

4 Return to the composite channel and keep the selection active. Choose Filter➡Render➡Lighting Effects. Select the Chrome style from the menu or match the settings in this figure. Make sure that there is plenty of gray in the preview. If your type appears washed out, the light is too strong. Lower the Intensity to fix this problem.

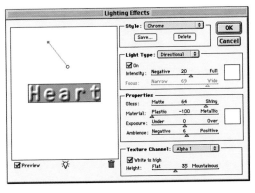

5 Deselect the selection and choose Filter➡Stylize➡Find Edges. This filter produces good contrasty highlights and shadows.

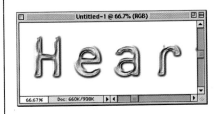

53

6 Choose Image➡Adjust➡ Curves. The Curves dialog box can be used to add subtle color to the chrome. From the menu at the top, select only one of the color channels (Blue). Then grab the line on the graph in the center and bend toward the upper-left corner to add a blue tint to the type and bend it toward the lower-right corner to make a warmer chrome.

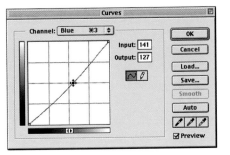

The final type with a drop shadow.

TIP

If you want to pick this type off the Background layer, load the Alpha 2 selection **and choose Select➡Modify➡Expand. Expand the selection enough to include most of the shadow areas to the lower right of the type (4 pixels). Choose Layer➡New➡Layer Via Cut to lift the type selection into a new layer.**

Gradient Chrome

1 Create a new file, create a new layer (Layer 1), and use the Type Mask tool to enter the text. (I used Poppl-Laudatio Bold Condensed at 110 points.) Save the selection to create the Alpha 1 channel.

2 Press Q to enter Quick Mask mode. Load the selection of the Quick Mask channel that has been temporarily added to the Channels palette. Then choose Select➡Modify➡Expand (6 pixels). The expand amount will be the thickness of the rim around the edge of the type.

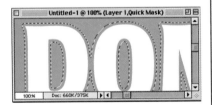

3 Choose Image➡Adjust➡Invert. Press Q to exit Quick Mask mode. Only a thin border around the type will be selected.

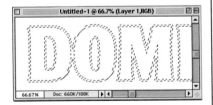

4 Choose 50% gray for the foreground color and fill the selection. Deselect the selection and then do Steps 2 through 5 on page ?? to turn the rim into chrome.

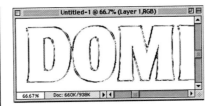

5 Load the Alpha 1 selection and double-click on the Linear Gradient tool. From the Gradient pop-up menu on the Linear Gradient Options palette select Chrome.

6 Hold the Shift key as you drag from the top of the type to the bottom of the type.

7 To finish I added a drop shadow and a couple of highlights (see page 102).

VARIATIONS

After selecting the Chrome gradient in Step 5, click the Edit button on the Linear Gradient Options palette. In the Gradient Editor dialog box that opens, you can change the colors in the gradient. ●

CLAY

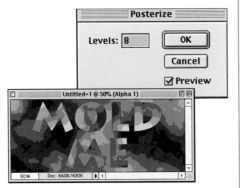

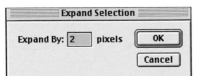

Another texture effect, clay, is created
by manipulating the lights and darks
in a channel used by the Lighting
Effects filter as a texture map.

1 Create a new file, and create a
new channel (Alpha 1). Use the
Type tool to enter the text. The
type in this example is Lithos Black
at 80 points.

2 Save the selection to create the
Alpha 2 channel. Deselect the type.

3 Then choose Filter➡Render➡
Difference Clouds to fill the channel (Alpha 1).

4 Choose Image➡Adjust➡
Posterize. Keep the setting low. I
used 8 levels. This step flattens the
cloud gradation into flat areas that
look like scraped clay.

5 Then choose Filter➡Render➡
Difference Clouds again. This is the
channel that will be used for the
clay texture.

6 Return to the composite channel,
and load the selection from the
Alpha 2 channel. Choose Select➡
Modify➡Expand (2 pixels). Expanding the selection eventually gives
the type its lip.

7 Choose Filter➡Render➡Lighting Effects. You can choose Clay from the Style menu or match the settings in this figure. Make sure to select Alpha 1 in the Texture Channel.

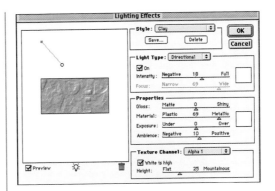

8 Keep the selection active and choose Image➡Adjust➡Auto Levels. This command automatically balances the lights and darks in the image.

9 Then choose Image➡Adjust➡ Hue/Saturation. Check the Colorize box and try these settings.

Deselect the text and dig in.

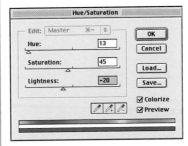

TIP If you want to put this type into its own layer, choose Layer➡New➡Layer Via Cut after Step 9.

Photoshop 5.0's new built-in drop shadow feature makes this effect simpler than ever. The second version here takes advantage of another of the new layer effects, Inner Bevel, to create cutout type with beveled edges.

1 Open a file with an image in it. This is a good time to take advantage of the stock photography included on the *Type Magic* CD-ROM. I opened the MM_0353.TIF image from the Vivid Details collection and cropped a part of it to fit into this 5-inch by 2-inch image.

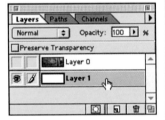

2 Double-click on the Background layer (the layer that contains the image) to open the Make Layer dialog box. The name defaults to Layer 0. Click OK. The background layer becomes Layer 0, which enables you to create a new layer (Layer 1), and move it below Layer 0.

3 Make Layer 0 invisible, choose a foreground color (I used white) for the underlying layer and fill Layer 1 with the color.

4 Make Layer 0 visible and make it the active layer. Use the Type Mask tool to enter the text. This is Triplex at 85 points.

5 Press Delete to clear the image from the type selection and reveal the contents of Layer 1.

6 All there is left to do is to use Photoshop's Layer Effect's Drop Shadow feature. Choose Layer➡ Effects➡Drop Shadow. Use any settings that suit you, keeping an eye on the image to check the results.

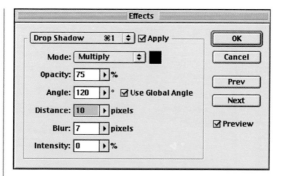

Beveled Cutout

Complete all previous steps. I cropped part of the MM_0004.TIF image from the P5TM CD-ROM to use with this effect.

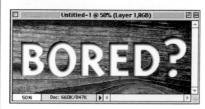

1 Create a new layer (Layer 2) and move the new layer above Layer 0, and load the transparency selection from Layer 0. Choose Select➡ Inverse and Select➡Modify➡ Expand (5 pixels).

2 Choose 50% gray for the foreground color and fill the selection. Deselect the selection.

59

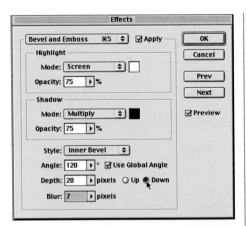

3 Choose Layer➡Effects➡Bevel and Emboss. Choose Inner Bevel, set the Angle so that it comes from the upper left (120°), and set the Depth to the maximum number of pixels (20) and Down. Set the Blur to 7 pixels.

TIP Balancing the Expand amount in Step 1 and the Blur amount in Step 3 is the most crucial element of this technique. If the Expand amount is too high relative to the Blur amount, the image will look as if the beveled surface ends before it reached the inner edge of the letters. If it is too low, there will be some odd light and dark areas around the inner edge of the bevel that will ruin the cutout illusion. Keep the settings near the 5 to 7 ratio used in this example.

4 Choose Layer➡Effects➡Create Layers. Two new layers show up in the Layers palette above Layer 2: one for the bevel shadows and one for the bevel highlights.

5 Make Layer 2 invisible, and then hold the (Option) [Alt] key and click on the dotted line just above Layer 2.

The bevel should now be in place.

TIP If you need to clean up the edges, load the transparency selection from Layer 0, and choose Select➡ Inverse. Make the Layer 2's Inner Bevel Highlights layer active and press Delete. Do the same for the Layer 2's Inner Bevel Shadows layer.

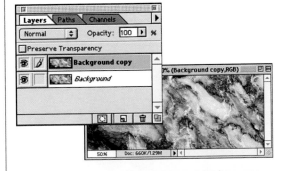

VARIATIONS

You can float the cutout type on top of itself by making these alterations to the steps that begin on page 59. Instead of Steps 2 and 3, duplicate the Background layer to create the Background copy layer and make this new layer the active layer for Steps 4 through 6.

After Step 6, make the Background layer the active layer and choose Image➡Adjust➡Brightness/ Contrast. Lower the Brightness (-20) to help set the Background layer back. ●

Photoshop contains a virtual arsenal of features that you can use to distress type. This technique does some fancy selection manipulations using the Quick Mask feature to distress type without using any channels.

I Create a new file and create a new layer (Layer 1). Use the Type Mask tool to enter the text (Futura Extra Bold at 75 points).

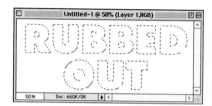

2 Press Q to enter Quick Mask mode. The area outside of the type selection turns red. Quick Mask mode creates a temporary channel that can be used to manipulate a selection. Choose Filter➡Brush Strokes➡Spatter. This filter distorts the edges of the type. In the preview, you can see the results of the settings you use. I set the Spray Radius and the Smoothness both at 5.

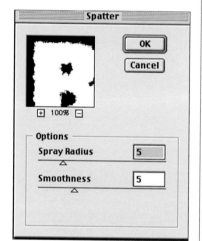

3 Press Q again to exit Quick Mask mode. The marching ants appear again, but now run around the rough edges created by the Spatter filter. Choose a foreground color for the type and fill the selection. Deselect the selection.

4 We're not done with the type or the Quick Mask mode. Press Q again. Then choose Filter➡ Render➡Clouds. The lighter areas seen here will end up being the areas that are rubbed out. If you don't like what the Clouds filter came up with, undo it and press (Command-F) [Control-F] to reapply the Clouds filter. I also made Layer I invisible in order to see the Quick Mask channel better.

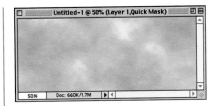

5 Choose Filter➡Noise➡Add Noise (50, Gaussian). Add a medium amount of noise. Don't obliterate what the Clouds filter did, but the noise should be very visible.

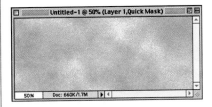

6 Choose Filter➡Pixelate➡ Pointillize and keep the Cell size low (3 pixels).

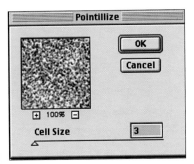

It appears as though the graininess from the Noise filter has been bloated.

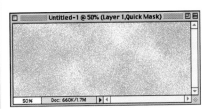

7 Choose Filter➡Pixelate➡ Fragment. A pattern will be created in the texture.

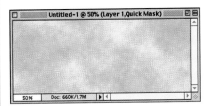

63

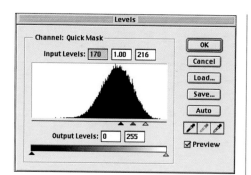

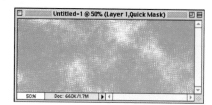

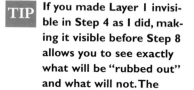

8 Then choose Image➡Adjust➡ Levels. As mentioned in Step 4, the light areas of the Quick Mask channel are the areas where the type will be rubbed out. In order to reduce the white areas, slide the black slider to the right, the white slider to the left, and then adjust the gray slider for fine-tuning. Adjusting these sliders gives you greater control over the white areas of the mask.

Click OK when you're satisfied.

TIP **If you made Layer 1 invisible in Step 4 as I did, making it visible before Step 8 allows you to see exactly what will be "rubbed out" and what will not. The areas where there is no red will be deleted.**

9 Press Q again to exit Quick Mask mode, and make Layer 1 visible if it is not. Press Delete to distress the type. Deselect the selection.

VARIATIONS

You can vary this technique at almost any stage to create unique distressing effects. The first variation creates two more selections using the Quick Mask feature in order to add two more colors to the distressed type.

Multicolor

After completing all the preceding steps, repeat Steps 4 through 8. Press Q to exit Quick Mask mode, and choose Image➡Adjust➡ Hue/Saturation. Use one or all the sliders to adjust the color of the selection. Here are the three stages of this type.

Texture

Use Photoshop 5.0's new Inner Bevel layer effect to add some texture to this effect. After completing the Multicolor variation, choose Layer➡Effects➡Bevel and Emboss and match the setting seen here...

...to get here. ●

65

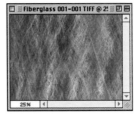

This technique demonstrates how to use an image (found on the P5TM CD-ROM) to help create a unique texture.

1 Choose File➡Open. Find the Fiberglass image in the D'pix collection on the P5TM CD-ROM (P5TM➡Images➡D'Pix➡Medium Resolution➡Fiberglass). When the Fiberglass image is open, choose Select➡All. Copy the image and close the file.

2 In a new file, create a new channel (Alpha 1), and paste the image into the channel. Because the image has been pasted into a channel, the color will be stripped away leaving a grayscale image. Choose Filter➡Sharpen➡Sharpen and deselect the selection.

3 Then choose Filter➡Other➡ High Pass. This filter flattens the image. The lower the Radius value, the less detail is retained. I used a radius value of 1.5 pixels for this effect. Deselect the selection.

4 Return to the composite channel and use the Type Mask tool to enter the text. (I used Compacta at 90 points.) Choose Select➡Feather (2 pixels). Feathering the selection causes the texture to appear to fade into the background.

66

TOOLBOX

Fiberglass (D´Pix Image)

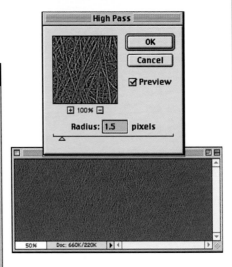

5 Then intersect the text selection with the selection from the Alpha 1 channel. Fill the selection with black and deselect the selection.

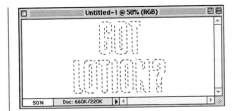

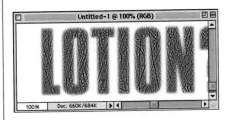

6 To enhance the texture, choose Image➡Adjust➡Levels. You can play around with these settings, but I found that Input Levels of: 0, .70, 189 worked well for this effect.

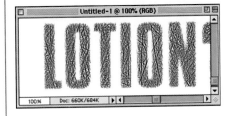

7 To add a bit of color, but not too much, I converted the image to Grayscale (Image➡Mode➡ Grayscale) and then to a duotone (Image➡Mode➡Duotone), using PANTONE Coated 441 as ink 1 and PANTONE Coated 411 as ink 2.

VARIATIONS

After pasting the fiberglass image into the Alpha 1 channel, choose Filter➡Brush Strokes➡Accent Edges. Enter an Edge Width of 1, an Edge Brightness of 50, and a Smoothness of 15. Skip to Step 4 and continue. Instead of doing Step 7, choose Image➡Adjust➡ Hue/Saturation and check the Colorize box (Hue: 51, Saturation: 49, Lightness: 0).

For more variations, try applying different filters to the Alpha 1 channel, as in the previous variation. For this effect, I chose Filter➡ Pixelate➡Fragment. ●

Blue Flame
(Color Table)

This classic effect builds the flames in a grayscale file and converts the image to a color mode that uses a special palette.

1 Create a new grayscale file. Choose black for the foreground color and fill the image with black.

2 Choose white as the foreground color and use the Type Mask tool to enter the text. For best results, use a heavy typeface (I used Hobo at 75 points). Move the type selection near the bottom of the image so there is room for flames to grow upward. Fill the type selection with white.

3 Save the selection to create the Alpha I channel, and deselect the selection.

4 Choose Image➡Rotate Canvas➡ 90° CCW. This temporary rotation is necessary in order to pull the flames upward. The image needs to be rotated because the Wind filter used in the next step only works horizontally.

5 Choose Filter➡Stylize➡Wind (Blast, From the Left). This filter pulls white streaks to the left of the type. The Method setting depends on the size of your type. Smaller type may need only Wind, whereas larger type may require the Blast feature applied twice.

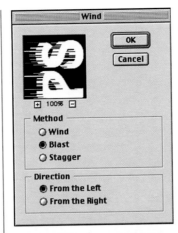

6 Choose Image➡Rotate➡90° CW to return the image to its original orientation.

7 Choose Filter➡Stylize➡Diffuse (Normal) in order to break the lines created by the Wind filter.

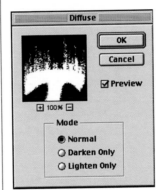

8 Choose Filter➡Blur➡Gaussian Blur (2.5 pixels). Set the Radius just high enough to smooth out the flames.

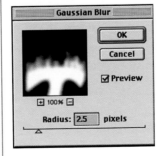

The type image should now look like this.

9 Choose Filter➡Distort➡Ripple (100, Medium) to add a little waviness to the type and flames.

10 Load the selection of the Alpha 1 channel, and choose Select➡Modify➡Contract (3 pixels). Adjust the Contract amount so that the interior of the type is selected and a thin wavy border is not selected. Choose Select➡Feather (1 pixel) to soften the selection. Then choose black as the foreground color and fill the selection. Deselect the selection.

TIP If you want the interior outlines of the type to also appear wavy (as in the "Flaming" thumbtab image), do Step 10 before Step 9.

11 Choose Image➡Mode➡Indexed Color to convert the grayscale file to indexed color, choose Image➡Mode➡Color Table, and choose Black Body from the Table menu.

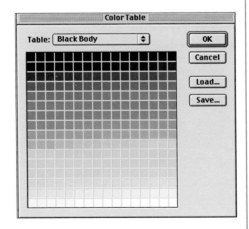

Just like the title of the book says: Magic!

 TIP You can adjust the Input Levels in the Levels dialog box to fine-tune the color and height of the flames. Choose Image➥Adjust➥ Levels.

VARIATIONS

The variations for this effect are countless. Here are a few I have gathered.

Blue Flames

Before Step 11, choose Image➥ Adjust➥Levels and set the Output Levels white slider to 190. Then choose Image➥Adjust➥Invert. In the Color Table dialog box in Step 11, click the Load button and find the Blue Flame color table on the P5TM CD-ROM (P5TM➥P5TM Files➥Miscellaneous➥Blue Flame).

Glass Texture

After completing Step 10, choose Filter➥Distort➥Glass. Set the Texture to Frosted (100% Scaling). You don't want to distort the type beyond recognition. Try some moderate settings such as Distortion: 2, Smoothness: 3.

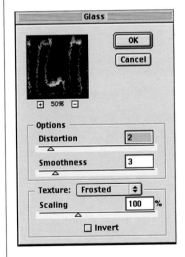

Do Step 11 to finish it off.

Fiery Clouds

In a new grayscale file (white background), choose black as the foreground color and use the Type Mask tool to enter the text. Fill the selection, and save the selection (Alpha 1). Deselect the text and choose Filter➡Blur➡Gaussian Blur (5 pixels). Load the Alpha 1 selection and fill it with black. Deselect the text, and choose Filter➡Render➡Difference Clouds. Do Step 11 to complete the effect.

Adding Swirls

Before Step 11, select the Elliptical Marquee tool and make a small selection around the flames of one letter.

Choose Filter➡Distort➡Twirl and adjust the Twirl amount to add swirls to the flames.

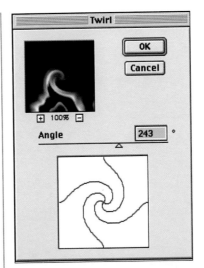

Continue selecting and twirling. ●

Displacement maps can seem confusing to the new user, but this effect makes simple use of them for some fun distortions. A displacement map is a second Photoshop file that is used to distort an image according to the gray values in the displacement map. You will never see the actual map when applying the Distort filter—Photoshop does all the work behind the scenes. However, for the following effects, I provide some peeks into the custom displacement maps that have been created for this effect. This effect is also easy to use on other effects.

1 Use the Type tool to enter the text, or place a type image in a layer. Make sure to leave some room around the edges of the type because some of these distortions significantly move the type in all directions. I used Seagull Heavy at 50 points. Choose Layer➡Type➡ Render Layer.

2 Deselect any active selections and choose Filter➡Distort➡ Displace. The dialog box enables you to control the intensity of the distortions. For this example, I set both Scale values to 10% (Stretch to Fit, Repeat Edge Pixels).

 TIP **You can also use negative values to inverse the distortions.**

74

3 Another dialog box appears asking you to select a displacement map. Included on the P5TM CD-ROM are several displacement maps that I have created for this effect. I chose Waving Line for this example (P5TM CD➡P5TM Files➡ Funhouse Displacement Maps➡ Waving Line).

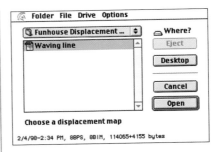

Here's the distorted type...

...and here she is after a couple of modifications.

TIP
You can create your own displacement maps to use with the displace filter. Open the files in the Funhouse Displacement Maps folder on the CD-ROM to look at the ones used for these effects. Any Photoshop file can be used as a displacement map, but keeping them simple is your best bet. Here is the displacement map (Waving Line) used on the Bearded Lady.

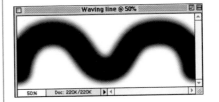

75

VARIATIONS

Here are a few more images indicating the displacement map (found on the P5TM CD-ROM) and settings used.

Offset Blurred Circles (Horizontal Scale: 10%, Vertical Scale: 18%)

X Polar B Displace (Horizontal
Scale: 15%, Vertical Scale: 10%) ●

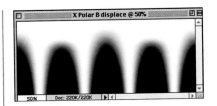

and tigers, too

The Glass filter used in this technique does a great job of creating realistic distortions if properly set up. The highlights are created through the aid of layer effects and the Curves feature.

1 Open a file that contains an image to be used as the background. I opened this file from the P5TM CD-ROM (P5TM➡Images➡Vivid Details➡MM_0266.TIF). Choose Select➡All, copy the image, and deselect the selection.

2 Create a new channel (Alpha 1) and use the Type tool to enter the text. (I used Bauhaus at 95 points.) Use the Move tool to position the type and save the selection to create the Alpha 2 channel.

3 Keep the selection active and choose Filter➡Blur➡Gaussian Blur (6 pixels). Blur the inside of the type enough to appear slightly rounded.

4 From the Channels palette menu, choose Duplicate Channel. In the dialog box that opens, select New from the Document menu and name the file (GlasText).

5 The channel opens as a new file. Save the file (Photoshop format) and close it.

6 Return to the composite channel, deselect the selection, and choose Filter➡Distort➡Glass. From the Texture menu, choose Load Texture and find the file that was saved in Step 4 (GlasText). Keep the settings close to what I used (Distortion: 7, Smoothness: 5), although you can vary them if you want a little less or more distortion.

This is one of the filters that does a great job of producing what it promises.

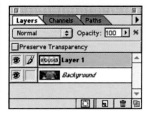

7 Load the Alpha 2 selection and choose Layer➡New➡Layer Via Copy to raise a copy of the distorted areas into a new layer (Layer 1). Make the Background layer active, choose Select➡All, and paste in the original image. Choose Merge Down from the Layers palette menu, and make Layer 1 the active layer again.

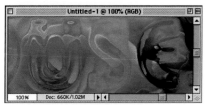

8 Choose Layer➡Effects➡Drop Shadow. Adding a shadow helps separate the glass from the background, but if you don't want it, skip this step and go on. I used the default settings, raised the Distance to 10, the Blur to 8, and the Intensity to 10%.

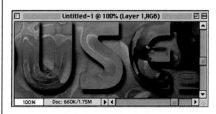

9 Create a new layer (Layer 2) and load the Alpha 2 selection. Choose 50% gray for the foreground color and fill the selection. Deselect the selection.

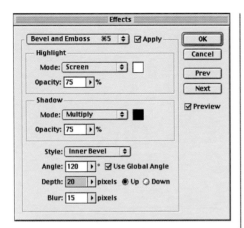

10 Choose Layer➡Effects➡Bevel and Emboss. Select Inner Bevel from the Style menu and raise the Depth to the maximum—20 pixels. Raise the Blur amount until the text appears rounded (15 pixels).

11 Choose Layer➡Effects➡Create Layers. Two new layers are added above Layer 2—one for the bevel highlights and one for the shadows. Choose Merge Group from the Layers palette menu to merge the beveled type back into a single layer (Layer 2).

12 Choose Image➡Adjust➡Curves and click on the Load button. Find the Chrome Curves file on the P5TM CD-ROM (P5TM➡P5TM Files➡Curves➡Chrome Curves). A wavy line is loaded into the graph that produces some wavy patterns inside the type.

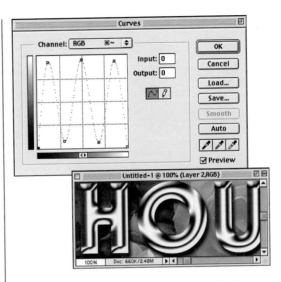

13 Change the Layer 2 blending mode to Overlay and double-click on the Layer 2 name to open the Layer Options dialog box. Slide the black slider below the This Layer gradient bar to the right—to about 25. Then hold the (Option) [Alt] key and click on the same slider. The slider will split in half. Drag the right half to the right. Watch the preview as the dark areas disappear from the type. I set this marker at 150.

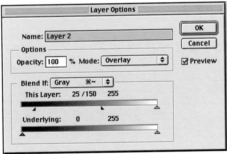

Getting rid of the dark areas greatly helps the glass highlights.

TIP **Depending on the colors in the underlying image, the glass type may look better if you invert Layer 2. Choose Image➡Adjust➡ Invert.**

14 To add just a touch of color to the glass, choose Image➡Adjust➡ Curves, select Blue from the Channel pop-up menu, and bend the line on the graph toward the upper-left corner. You can skip this step, but I find that it helps to separate the glass from the background.

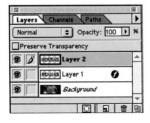

VARIATIONS

Ridge

If you don't like the way the type meets the background and want to add a ridge around the letters, add these steps. If you've already gone through all of the steps, use the History palette to revert back through the effect.

In Step 7, after loading the selection, choose Select➡Modify➡ Expand (4 pixels). Set the Expand amount to the desired thickness of the edge that runs around the letters. Finish Step 7 and Steps 8 through 11; then add these steps.

Create a new layer (Layer 3) and load the selection of the Alpha 2 channel. Choose Select➡Modify➡ Expand. Set the Expand amount to same amount that you used before. Then subtract from the selection the selection of the Alpha 2 channel. There should now be a thin selection that surrounds all of the letters.

Choose 50% gray for the foreground color and fill the selection. Then choose Layer➡Effects➡Bevel and Emboss. Select the Inner Bevel style and adjust the Depth (5 pixels) and Blur (5 pixels) to round the gray border. The default settings worked well here.

Perform the Step 11 commands on this layer and choose Merge Down to merge Layers 2 and 3.

Deselect the selection and complete Steps 12 through 14.

Colored Glass

Create a new layer and move the layer above all other layers. Load the Alpha 2 selection. If you added the ridge to the glass, choose Select➡Modify➡Expand and expand the selection the same amount as you did in the first step of the Ridge variation. Choose a foreground color for the color of the glass (CMYK: 75, 0, 100, 0) and fill the selection. Bright colors work best. Change the layer blending mode to Color. ●

Glossy (Lighting
Effects Style)

Here are two quick ways to make great-looking glossy type. The first uses a displacement map to help make the textured type look rounded, and the second adds a glossy effect to solid-colored type.

1 Texture is used in this effect because it emphasizes the round-ness of the type as the texture wraps around it. The first step is to find a texture to use. I used KPT Texture Explorer plug-in to gener-ate a texture, but you might simply place an image inside a type mask. If you're going to use an image, open the file now and choose Select➡ All. Copy the image and close the file. Several images are located on the CD-ROM that you might use. Follow this path to find them: P5TM CD-ROM➡P5TM Files➡ Textures. If you're not using an image, begin with Step 2.

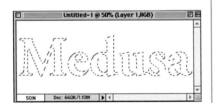

2 Create a new layer (Layer 1), and use the Type Mask tool to enter the text. This is Adobe Garamond Bold at 110 points.

3 The next step is to fill the type with a texture, pattern, or image. If you use an image, choose Edit➡ Paste Into and go on to Step 3.1 used a texture provided by the KPT Texture Explorer (Filters➡ KPT➡KPT Texture Explorer).

4 Save the selection as a new channel (Alpha 1). Duplicate the channel to create the Alpha 1 copy channel. Make Alpha 1 copy the active channel.

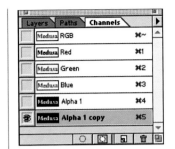

5 Keep the selection active and choose Filter➡Blur➡Gaussian Blur. The amount that you blur the type is the most crucial step in this effect. The blur will eventually affect the way that the Lighting Effects filter works in Step 9. Set the radius so that your type looks something like what I created here. (I used 6 pixels.) If you blur the letters too much, the edges will look beveled rather than rounded. The blur should be smoothly applied inside the letters.

6 Choose Duplicate Channel from the Channels palette menu. Select new from the Document menu, name the file (Medusa Displace), and click OK. When the new file opens, save it and close it. This new file becomes the displacement map used in Step 7 that tells Photoshop how to distort the image.

7 Return to the composite channel, choose Select➡All, and Filter➡Distort➡Displace. Adjust the Scale percentages to control the roundness of the letters. I set them both at 5%. If you choose values too high, the effect won't work, so keep it low.

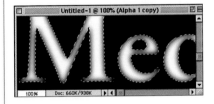

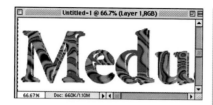

8 A new dialog box opens asking you to find a displacement map. Find the file that you saved in Step 7 (Medusa Displace) and click Open. The distortion is subtle, but it's enough to aid in getting the type to appear rounded.

9 To get rid of the underlying copy of the type that the Displace filter created, load the selection from the Alpha 1 channel, and choose Select➡Inverse and press Delete.

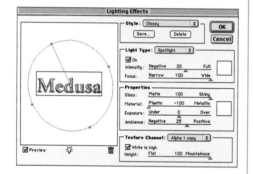

10 Deselect the selection, choose Filter➡Render➡Lighting Effects, and either select the Glossy preset, match the settings seen here, or choose your own.

11 Finally, choose Filter➡Artistic➡ Plastic Wrap. You might need to experiment to find the right settings, but try these first: Highlight Strength: 10, Detail: 15, Smoothness: 15.

Glossy

The Plastic Wrap filter does a nice job of polishing off the glossy finish.

TIP **The Plastic Wrap filter produces very different results depending upon the size of the area selected. If you don't like the results you got from Step 10, try selecting only one or a few letters at a time and applying the filter. This technique is used in the following Solid Color Glossy section.**

Solid Color Glossy

1 Create a new layer, set the foreground color to black, and use the Type Mask tool to enter the text (Thickhead at 125 points). Fill the type selection with black. Save the selection as a new channel (Alpha 1).

2 Choose Select➡Feather and set the amount to approximately 5 pixels. The corners of the "running ants" adjust only slightly.

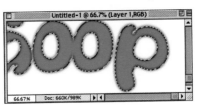

3 Set the foreground color to a color for the type (I used CMYK: 75, 0, 100, 0), and fill the feathered selection. This two-color fill tricks the Plastic Wrap filter into finding the highlights that you want.

87

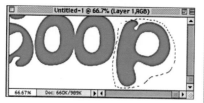

4 To get rid of the extra color outside the selection, load the selection of the Alpha 1 channel, choose Select➡Inverse, and press Delete. Deselect the selection.

5 Use the Rectangular Marquee tool or the Lasso tool to select only one of the letters. The Plastic Wrap filter provides drastically different effects depending on how much area is selected. I have found that selecting only one letter at a time gives me just the right highlights when trying to make that glossy look.

6 Choose Filter➡Artistic➡Plastic Wrap. For solid colors, this filter does all of the work to create the glossy effect. Play with the settings, but try these first: Highlight Strength: 9, Detail: 9, Smoothness: 13.

7 Repeat Steps 5 and 6 for each letter.

The Gradient tool can do so much more than fill a type selection with a preset gradient. Following are several techniques that show you how to get a little more out of this powerful tool.

Basic Gradient

Use the layer blending modes to map a gradient onto existing type.

1 To create this type, choose 50% gray for the foreground color and use the Plastic effect from the Raised section (page 146).

2 Select any Gradient tool. Find the Gradient Options palette and select a preset gradient from the pop-up menu. Set the blending mode to Color.

3 Click and drag the Gradient tool across the type.

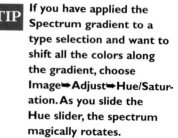

The gradient colors blend right over the raised type.

> **TIP** If you have applied the Spectrum gradient to a type selection and want to shift all the colors along the gradient, choose Image➡Adjust➡Hue/Saturation. As you slide the Hue slider, the spectrum magically rotates.

Layering Gradients

By stacking two layers filled with gradients, you can create new gradients using the layer blending modes.

1 Use the Type tool to enter the text. (I used Informal Black at 110 points.) Choose Layer➡Type➡ Render Layer and turn on the Preserve Transparency option.

2 Select the Linear Gradient tool and find the Linear Gradient Options palette. Select a multicolored gradient from the pop-up menu or create your own. I chose the Spectrum gradient.

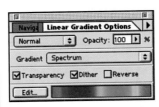

3 Click and drag the gradient across the type.

4 Duplicate the type layer and turn on the Preserve Transparency option for this layer, too. Also, set the layer blending mode to Difference. The type turns black.

91

5 Use the Linear Gradient tool and drag it across the type in a different direction.

6 Repeat Steps 4 and 5 to create a third layer. Be sure to drag the gradient in a new direction from Step 5.

7 I applied an Outer Bevel to finish the type.

VARIATIONS

Perform Step 1, create a new layer (Layer 1), select the Radial Gradient tool, and then select Transparent Rainbow gradient. Click and drag many gradients to cover the type. Set the Layer 1 blending mode to Overlay. Group this layer with the type layer.

Then duplicate Layer 1 (Layer 1 copy) and choose Filter➡Other➡ Offset (Horizontal: 20 pixels, Vertical: 20 pixels). Set the Layer 1 copy blending mode to Color. Then duplicate Layer 1 again (Layer 1 copy 2) and choose Filter➡ Other➡Offset (Horizontal: -20 pixels, Vertical: -20 pixels). Set the Layer 1 copy 2 blending mode to Difference. Finally, group all the gradient layers with the type layer.

 A shortcut to creating your own gradients: Select and use one of Photoshop 5.0's built-in gradients and then choose Image➡Adjust➡ Hue/Saturation. Use the Hue slider to run through a store of new gradients.

Graded Selections

You can also use the Gradient tool to make graded selections enabling you to blend images together. Try this technique for blending two photographs into a type selection.

1 Create a new file and use the Type Mask tool to enter the text (Triplex Extra Bold at 110 points). I also chose Select➡Transform Selection and used the handles to stretch the type selection to fill the document window. Save the selection (Alpha 1).

2 Open a file containing the image to be placed in the top half of the type (Adobe Photoshop 5.0➡ Extras➡Samples➡Big Sky). Choose Select➡All, copy the selection, and close the file.

3 Return to the file that contains the active selection and choose Edit➡Paste Into. The image will be pasted into a new layer (Layer 1) and the type selection will be turned into a layer mask. Use the Move tool to move the image around if desired.

4 Load the Alpha 1 selection and then press Q to enter Quick Mask mode. Select the Linear Gradient tool and find the Linear Gradient Options palette. Choose the Black, White gradient from the pop-up menu.

5 Load the selection of the Layer 1 Quick Mask (temporarily placed in the Channels palette). Then hold the Shift key and click and drag the Gradient tool from just above the center of the type to just above the bottom of the type. This blended quick mask represents the graded selection that you will have after exiting Quick Mask mode.

6 Press Q to exit Quick Mask mode. It will appear as if only half of the type is selected.

7 Again, open a file containing the image that you want to paste into the bottom of the type selection (MM_0266.TIF from Vivid Details). Choose Select➡All, copy it, and close the file.

8 Return to the type file and choose Edit➡Paste Into to paste the image into the graded selection. Again the image is pasted into a new layer (Layer 2) and the graded selection becomes the layer mask. Use the Move tool to position the image.

9 I used the Outer Bevel layer effect to finish the type.

VARIATIONS

After Step 8, deselect any selections. Click on the Layer 2 layer mask (on the Layers palette) to make it active and select the Linear Gradient tool (Black, White gradient). Click and drag the Gradient tool from the center of the type to just above the bottom of the type.

Piling up the Gradients

If you want to pile up several gradients in a single layer, you must make sure that the ends of the gradients are transparent.

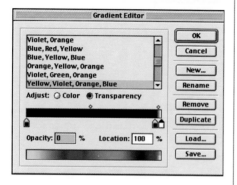

1 Select one of the gradients from the Gradient Options palette pop-up menu and click on the Edit button.

2 Then click on the Transparency radio button. Click just below the bar to create a new black slider. Position it a little to the left of the slider on the right (Location: 95%). Then click on the slider at the extreme right end of the bar. Change the Opacity to 0%. Click OK.

3 To try out this gradient, use the Type tool to enter the text (Cooper Black at 120 points). Choose Layer➡Type➡Render Layer. Choose Layer➡Effects➡ Bevel and Emboss. Select the Inner Bevel style, and set the Depth to 10 and the Blur to 10.

4 Turn on the Preserve Transparency option for the type layer. Select the Radial Gradient tool and go nuts—keep clicking and dragging to overlap many gradients of varying diameters.

More Variations

Press D to set the colors to their defaults; then choose Filter➡ Render➡Difference Clouds. Choose Image➡Adjust➡Invert. To fine-tune the colors, I used the Levels dialog box to increase the contrast and the Hue/Saturation dialog box to adjust the colors.

Just one more step:
Filter➡Stylize➡Find Edges. ●

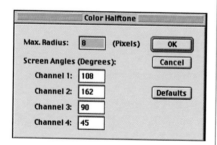

Creating halftoned type is a simple one-step technique, but you can create many great patterns by starting with the Hafltone filter and then applying various other Photoshop filters. Here are some examples:

1 Create a new file and use the Type tool to enter the text. (I used Benguiat at 90 points.) I set the color swatch in the Type tool dialog box to CMYK: 0, 75, 100, 0. Choose Layer➡Type➡Render Layer.

TIP The color that you choose for the type will make a big difference in the results, but the only way to find out what the Color Halftone filter will do with it is to try it out.

2 Choose Filter➡Pixelate➡Color Halftone. The channel settings in this dialog box correspond to the red, green, and blue channels of your file. Because only three channels are in an RGB file, the fourth angle setting is ignored. The Max. Radius limits the size of the circles that the filter creates. Try the default angles and set the Max. Radius to 8, a little above the minimum Max. setting.

98

That's the basic halftoned type.

 After applying the Color Halftone filter, choose Image➡Adjust➡Hue/Saturation and use the Hue slider to run through some other color choices.

VARIATIONS

Large Circles
Perform Steps 1 and 2. In Step 2, set the Max. Radius to 40.

Do Steps 1 and 2 and then choose Filter➡Render➡Difference Clouds. Then make only one of the color channels active (Green) and choose Filter➡Stylize➡Find Edges. Make the RGB channel active again and choose Filter➡Render➡Difference Clouds. Press (Command-F) [Control-F] to reapply the Difference Clouds filter. I also applied an Inner Bevel and a Drop Shadow.

Rippled
Perform Steps 1 and 2 and then choose Filter➡Distort➡Ripple (150, Medium).

Polka?

Polka?

Clouds

Do Steps 1 and 2; then choose Filter➡Noise➡Dust and Scratches (Radius: 8, Threshold: 168). Choose Filter➡Render➡Difference Clouds. Press (Command-F) [Control-F] to reapply the filter.

Clouds II

Complete the Clouds variation; then make a copy of the type layer and choose Layer➡Effects➡Clear Effects to clear the effects from the new layer. Choose Filter➡Render➡ Difference Clouds and change the layer blending mode to Difference.

Spilled-Over Dots

If you don't want to keep the edges contained within the type, choose Flatten Image from the Layers palette menu after Step 1. Complete Step 2.

Just Dots

Start with the Spilled-Over Dots variation; then load the selection of one of the color channels (Green). Choose Select➡Inverse. Create a new layer, choose a foreground color, and fill the selection. Delete the original type layer. I also applied an Inner Bevel and a Drop Shadow to the new layer. ●

Here are four ways to add a
sparkle to your type. Two of them
use filters, one uses a custom paintbrush, and the last uses the
Gradient tool. Choose your
weapon.

The Custom
Paintbrush

1 Open the file containing the type
to which you want to add highlights. This type was created with
the Gradient Chrome effect on
page 54.

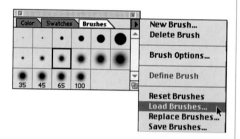

2 Find the Brushes palette and
choose Load Brushes from the
palette menu.

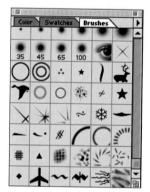

3 Follow this path to open the
Assorted Brushes file: Adobe
Photoshop 5.0➡Goodies➡Brushes
& Patterns➡Assorted Brushes. A
range of new brushes appear in
the Brushes palette.

4 Scroll to the bottom of the
palette and select this brush:

102

TIP **You can use the brush on either side of the brush I recommended for slightly different sparkles.**

5 Choose white (or another bright color) for the foreground color.

6 To add sparkles to the type, use the Paintbrush tool to click on the type where you want the sparkle. Don't drag the brush or you will smear the sparkle.

Sparkles, sparkles, sparkles.

TIP **To intensify a sparkle, click twice on the same spot, or make a small circling motion with the sparkle brush to spread and blur it.**

The Lens Flare

1 For this method, I started with this type created using the Reflector effect (page 46).

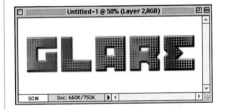

2 Choose Filter➡Render➡Lens Flare. In the dialog box preview, drag the flare to a spot on the type. I set the Brightness at 150%. Make sure that the Brightness percentage is not so high that you have all highlight and no type.

103

Click OK and you're finished.

The Gradient Highlight

1 This type was created using the Plastic effect on page 146.

2 Choose white for the foreground color or another color for the highlight.

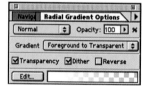

3 Double-click the Radial Gradient tool to select it and to open the Radial Gradient Options palette. Change the Gradient type to Foreground to Transparent.

4 Click on the Edit button. Then click on the Transparency button. The black bar represents the transparency, or opacity, of the gradient at each point along its transition. The gradient is 100% opaque if the bar is black. Grab the black marker and slide it to the right a little. This will slightly extend the completely opaque part of the radial gradient—near the center. Then grab the diamond on top and slide it to the left a little. This will make the gradient fade from opaque to transparent a little quicker. Click OK.

5 Create a new layer (Layer 1) and change the Layer 1 blending mode to Overlay. Click and drag with the Gradient tool from the point for the center of the highlight. Drag the Gradient line until it reaches as far as you want the highlight to spread. In this example, I dragged the Gradient tool from the center of the word to the end of the word.

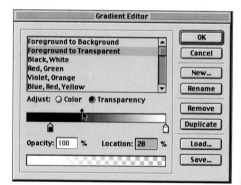

Lighting Effects Filter

In this technique, the highlights are actually added, using the Lighting Effects filter, to a new layer above the type. Then the layer is blended with the type layer.

1 I made some Plastic type for this filter (page 146).

2 Create a new layer above the layer containing the type and fill the layer with 50% gray or a lighter color. Then choose Filter➡ Render➡Lighting Effects. Add lights to the preview where you want highlights. I added just two lights in this example. Raise the Ambience slider enough to make sure that the gray away from the highlights remains relatively close to 50% gray.

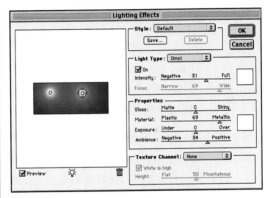

3 Change the layer blending mode to Overlay for the new layer. The highlights spill right onto the type. ●

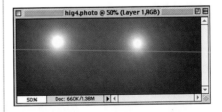

The Clouds filter, plus two others, help create this realistic marble from scratch.

1 Create a new file. Use the Type Mask tool to enter the text onto a white background. Marble looks good in a blocky font such as Machine (135 points).

2 Keep the selection active. Make sure that the foreground color is set to black and choose Filter➡Render➡Difference Clouds.

3 Reapply this filter a few times. The more times you apply the filter, the more the veins of the marble break up. I applied the Difference Clouds filter two times. Here is what my type looked like.

4 Choose Filter➡Stylize➡Find Edges. This filter pulls the veins out of the clouds.

5 Choose Image➡Adjust➡Invert.

6 Next, choose Image➡Adjust➡ Levels. Grab the white Input marker and slide it to the left until it sits under the beginning of the steep slope in the previous graph. Then nudge the gray input marker to the right. Watch the preview and use these two sliders to adjust the marbling.

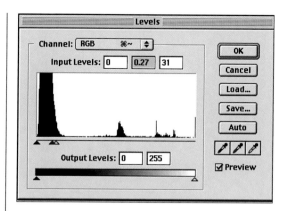

7 Choose Image➡Adjust➡ Hue/Saturation. Turn on the Colorize option. Then adjust the Saturation marker so that the color comes through but isn't too bright. I set it right in the middle, at 50. Use the Hue slider to find a color for the marble. For more color, nudge the Lightness up just a little.

8 The Find Edges filter leaves a funny edge on the type. Choose Select➡Modify➡Contract. Contract the selection 1 or 2 pixels—just enough so that the selection is inside the marble. I chose 2 pixels. Choose Select➡Inverse and press Delete to fill the background with white. ●

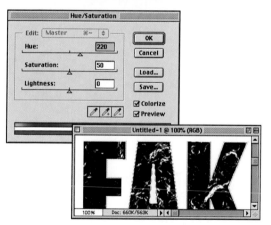

This technique uses some of Photoshop's most basic filters to create a simple, effective, and oh so speedy type treatment.

1 Create a new file, and choose a foreground color for the type (CMYK: 100, 0, 100, 40). Use the Type tool to enter the text (Futura Bold at 75 points). Use a typeface that is heavy enough that it won't be obliterated by the Wind filter used in Step 4. Choose Layer➡Type➡Render Layer. This is another effect that you can apply to any type image as long as it is merged into a single layer.

2 Choose Filter➡Stylize➡Wind (Wind, From the Right). The filter will not create prominent streaks, but the streaks will be enough to give the Motion Blur filter something to work with.

3 To improve the illusion of movement, use the Smudge tool to lengthen some of the streaks. You can skip this step if you want to, but a few smudges can greatly improve the effect. Double-click the Smudge tool to select it and bring the Smudge Options palette to the front. Set the Pressure to 50% (Normal). Choose a soft-edged brush from the Brushes palette, and drag on the back edges of the type. Hold Shift while dragging to keep the smudging perfectly horizontal.

4 Choose Filter➡Blur➡Motion Blur (10 pixels). Set the angle to 0° so the blur remains absolutely horizontal. You can raise the Distance setting, but don't go too crazy or the tortoise will look like he's just standing there shaking.

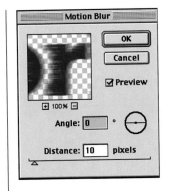

5 Choose Filter➡Stylize➡Wind (Wind, From the Right) again. After smudging and blurring, applying this filter a second time has a greater impact.

TIP If applying the Wind filter in Step 5 washes away too much of the type, choose Filter➡Fade Wind and lower the percentage. I did that here and set the percentage at 75%.

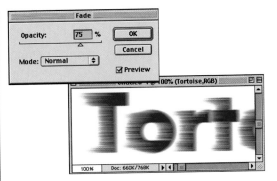

6 Choose Filter➡Sharpen➡ Unsharp Mask (Amount: 75, Radius: 4, Threshold: 3) to sharpen the edges that became a little too blurry after applying the Motion Blur filter.

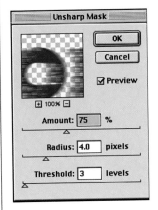

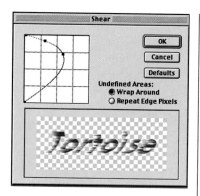

7 Choose Filter➡Distort➡Shear. This filter distorts the type according to how you distort the line in the 4 × 4 grid. Grab the line in the middle to add a point to it and drag it up to the position of the lower point in this figure. Then pull both of the top and bottom points all the way to the left. Finally, I added another point higher up on the curve to fine-tune the bend.

TIP **Here is another good place to use the Smudge tool to lengthen and smooth the streaks.**

8 Choose Filter➡Distort➡ Spherize. This final distortion bloats the type in the center, making it look a little like it is rounding a corner. I set the Amount to 50% (Normal).

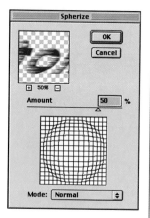

The settings used for all the filters used in this effect might be varied in order to create slightly different effects.

VARIATIONS

Quick Fix
If all you want to do is put a quick swerve in your type, use the Shear filter. Do Step 1 and then Step 7. Here is the Shear filter dialog box.

And here is the result.

Shadow
To add a shadow beneath the type, choose Layer➡Effects➡Drop Shadow (Mode: Multiply, Opacity: 50%, Angle: 0°, Distance: 20 pixels, Blur: 20 pixels, Intensity: 0%). Then choose Layer➡Effects➡Create Layer. A new layer that contains the shadow will be created below the type layer. Make the new layer active. Choose Edit➡Transform➡ Scale; grab the top center handle while holding the Shift key and pull it straight down to condense the shadow.

Press (Return) [Enter] to accept the transformation, and use the Move tool to shift the shadow down and to the left of the type. Then choose Filter➡Blur➡ Gaussian Blur (1 pixel) to smooth the shadow out a little. ●

111

Those fantastic glowing tubes are created with some fancy selections, a couple of color fills, the new Outer Glow layer effect, and the Plastic Wrap filter. A couple of quick methods are shown in the Variations.

1 Create a new file; then choose black for the foreground color and fill the Background layer with black. The only way to achieve that radiant neon glow is to contrast the bright color of the type against a dark background color. You don't have to use black, but make sure that the color you choose is significantly darker than the color of the type.

2 Use the Type Mask tool to enter the text. (I used VAG Rounded at 100 points.) If you have the VAG Rounded typeface, use it; the roundness of this typeface makes creating the tubes a little easier. If you don't, choose a heavy block typeface, choose Select➡Modify➡Smooth, and set the Radius high enough to round the corners of the type.

3 Press Q to enter Quick Mask mode. Here the type selection can quickly be changed into tubes. Load the selection of the Quick Mask (this channel has been temporarily placed in the Channels palette) and choose Select➡Modify➡Contract (8 pixels). Contract the selection enough so that you can see a good black border all the way around the outside of the selection.

112

4 Fill the contracted selection with black (it will actually fill with red because you're in Quick Mask mode, but use black as the foreground color), and deselect the selection. You can now see the tubes running all the way around the type.

5 Press Q again to exit Quick Mask mode. Choose a foreground color that is somewhat darker than the color you want to use for the neon (CMYK: 0, 75, 100, 40). The selection will be filled again in the next step with a brighter color. Fill the selection and save the selection (Alpha 1).

6 Choose Select➡Feather (3 pixels), choose a foreground color that is a brighter variation of the color used in the Step 4 (CMYK: 0, 0, 72, 0), and fill the selection.

 Depending upon the colors that you are using for the type, the RGB mode often displays brighter colors than the CMYK mode. These bright colors may turn into mud when you convert the image to CMYK mode later. If you plan to convert this file to CMYK mode and don't want to be surprised, convert the image now.

113

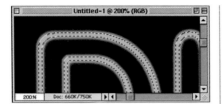

7 Load the selection of the Alpha 1 channel and choose Select➥ Modify➥Contract (2 pixels). After contracting the selection, the selection remains continuous through-out the letters. Choose Select➥Feather (1 pixel) to soften the selection just a bit.

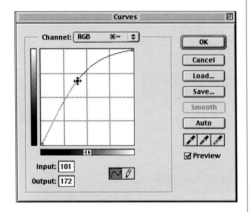

8 Choose Image➥Adjust➥Curves. Grab the center of the line in the graph and bend it up and to the left. Watch the image. The interior of the letters brighten and improve the look of the glow.

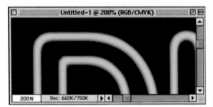

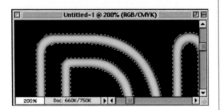

9 Load the selection of the Alpha 1 channel again; then choose Select➥Modify➥Expand (1 pixel). Expanding the selection just a little will pick up some of the darkness from the black background.

10 Choose Layer➡New➡Layer Via Cut to create a new layer (Layer 1) that includes only the tubes. Cutting the selection into a new layer leaves a "hole" in the Background layer. Removing the black from this part of the background helps to brighten the glow added in the next step.

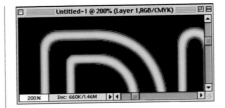

11 Choose Layer➡Effects➡Outer Glow. Choose a glow color that is close to the bright color chosen in Step 6 (CMYK: 0, 0, 72, 0). Set the Opacity to 100%; raise the Blur to about 20 pixels and the Intensity to around 10%. These settings should work well for you, but adjust them if necessary.

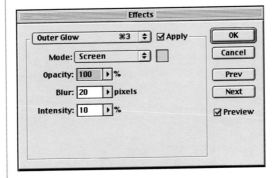

12 Choose Filter➡Artistic➡Plastic Wrap. This filter places some highlights that follow the shape of the tubes. Try these settings: Highlight Strength: 15, Detail: 9, Smoothness: 7. Because this filter can produce drastically different results depending on the image that is used, you will probably need to experiment with the settings to find the right highlights.

VARIATIONS

Quick Neon
Choose a bright foreground color for the neon text (CMYK: 72, 0, 36, 0), and use the Type tool to enter the text (VAG Rounded at 120 points). Load the transparency selection of the new type layer; then choose Flatten Image from the Layers palette menu.

Choose Select➡Inverse and Select➡Feather (6 pixels). The Feather amount determines the softness and extent of the glow.

Choose black (or another dark color) for the foreground color and fill the selection to complete the effect.

The Neon Glow Filter

Do Steps 2 through 4 on page 112 pand press Q to exit Quick Mask mode. Save the selection (Alpha 1). Choose black for the background color and choose a foreground color for the neon (CMYK: 72, 0, 36, 0). Fill the selection and then deselect the selection. Press X to switch the foreground and background colors; then choose Filter➡Artistic➡Neon Glow. Click on the color swatch to pick a color for the neon glow (CMYK: 100, 80, 0, 0) and adjust the settings to control the glow (Size: 17, Brightness: 35). Finally, load the selection of the Alpha 1 channel, choose Select➡Feather (1 pixel), and feather the selection a small amount. Press X again and fill the selection to complete the effect. ●

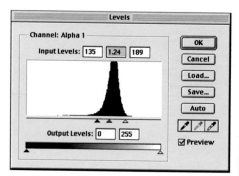

This technique uses information from a background image to control the texture of the type that is "painted" on top. The Paint Strokes variation adds a nice finishing touch to this effect.

1 Begin this effect with a textured background image like this image that was cropped and resized from the Photo 24 020 wall image on the P5TM CD-ROM (P5TM➡Images➡Photo 24➡Walls➡020). Some images work better than others. An image that is almost monochromatic and has an even distribution of texture, like this one, works well. Check out the variations to see what to do if the image is darker.

2 Choose Select➡All to select the entire background image, and copy it. Create a new channel (Alpha 1) and paste in the image. Deselect the selection.

3 Choose Image➡Adjust➡Levels. In the Levels dialog box, use the Input Levels sliders to adjust the darks and lights in this channel. The values in this channel act as a map for the painted type. Where this channel is light, the type will show through, and where this channel is dark, the background image will show through. You are looking for something that has some of each. Generally, you want to bring the two outside sliders (black and white) in toward the center. If you click the Auto button, it gets you close to what you're looking for. Then adjust the middle (gray) slider so that the image has a good dose of middle grays.

A good gray image such as the one seen here works great.

4 Choose Filter➡Noise➡Add Noise. Keep the setting low; add just enough noise so there is faint texture to the channel (20, Gaussian).

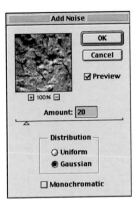

5 Return to the composite channel, create a new layer (Layer 1), and use the Type Mask tool to enter the text. I used AG Book Stencil at 105 points.

6 Intersect the type selection with the selection of the Alpha 1 channel. Then choose an approximate foreground color (CMYK: 0, 100, 75, 0) for the type and fill the selection. Deselect the selection.

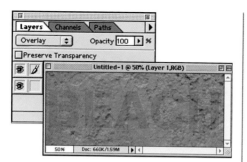

7 Change the Layer blending mode to Overlay. You might not need to change the Layer blending mode. For some images, Normal works better than Overlay (as in the last image on page 119). It depends upon the color of the type and the color or colors of the background. Try both and pick the one that works best. Don't worry too much about the color right now; it will be adjusted in the next step and again in Step 10.

8 Choose Image➡Adjust➡Hue➡Saturation. Check the Colorize option to turn it on, and watch the preview as you adjust the sliders to find the right color. You will probably need to raise the Saturation level quite a bit (I ended up with 100). If you can't get the type as dark as you want it, don't worry—we will darken it in Step 10.

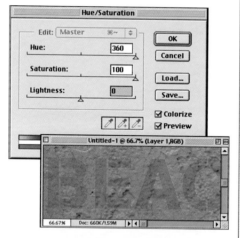

9 Choose Filter➡Stylize➡Diffuse (Normal) and Filter➡Distort➡Ripple (Amount: 135%, Size: Small). These filters roughen the type, especially at the edges.

10 Duplicate Layer 1 and move the new layer (Layer 1 copy) below Layer 1. Choose Image➡Adjust➡Levels. After Step 9, the type should have become brighter. To darken and strengthen the type while still letting the background texture show through, adjust the Input sliders. For this image, I brought the black slider almost all the way to the right.

Click OK and you're done.

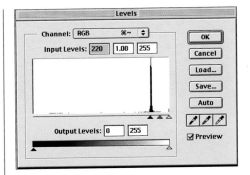

VARIATIONS

Paint Strokes
After completing all of the preceding steps, create a new layer (Layer 2) and move it above Layer 1. Load the transparency selection of Layer 1, choose black for the foreground color, and fill the selection. Then fill it two more times to darken it. Choose Filter➡Noise➡Add Noise (999, Gaussian, Monochromatic). Deselect the selection and choose Filter➡Blur➡Motion Blur. The angle set here will be the angle that the strokes run across the type. I set the Angle to -27°. Adjust the amount so that there are good streaks through the noise (26). Be careful not to set it too high or the blurring will wash everything out.

Set the Layer 2 blending mode to Luminosity—instant paint streaks. If the streaks are not subtle enough, lower the Opacity for Layer 2.

TIP **If you don't like the dark glow that this variation created around the type,** load the transparency selection **of Layer 1, choose Select➡Inverse, and press Delete to get rid of it.**

122

A Darker Background

As mentioned in Step 7, you might need to make adjustments to this technique for each unique combination of type color and background color. For this example, I used the TEXTR_27.PCT (Image Club) image from the P5TM CD-ROM (P5TM➠Images➠Image Club➠ Textures➠TEXTR_27.PCT) and followed all of the previous steps, except that I left the Layer 1 blending mode set at Normal, and I moved Layer 2 on top of Layer 1 and set its blending mode to Overlay.

 If you want to add a little thickness to the paint, as in the thumbtab image, dese-lect any selections, make Layer 1 copy active, **and nudge it one keystroke down and one keystroke to the right.** ●

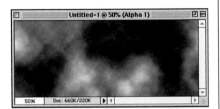

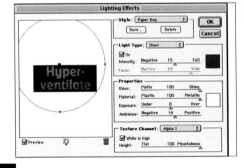

TOOLBOX

Paper Bag
(Lighting Effects
Style)

This technique demonstrates a quick-and-easy way to use the Clouds and Lighting Effects filters to create a brown paper bag texture. A quick change of color turns the texture into aluminum foil.

1 Create a new file. It must be an RGB file so that you can use the Lighting Effects filter. Create a new channel to hold the texture (Alpha 1), and choose Filter→Render→Clouds. The Alpha 1 channel should look like this.

2 Return to the composite channel, set the foreground color to white, and use the Type tool to enter the text. I used BadgerBold at 80 points. Choose Layer→Type→Render Layer. I made the background layer invisible so you can see the white type, barely.

3 Now, here's the magic step. Choose Filter→Render→Lighting Effects and choose Paper Bag from the Style menu, or match the settings as seen in this figure.

Click OK, and you are ready for lunch.

4 Okay, maybe not before a little fine-tuning. Choose Image➡ Adjust➡Levels. Bring the black and white sliders to the edges of the Input histogram (as shown). Then slide the white Output slider to the left just enough to take the sheen off of the texture.

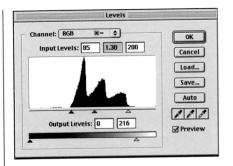

A shadow helped to set off the final image from the background.

Foil

By changing the color of the light in the Lighting Effects filter, you can use this same technique to create foil. Click on the Light Color box and set the values to CMYK: 27, 12, 15, 1.

TIP To fine tune the Foil, choose Image➡Adjust➡ Brightness/Contrast and raise the Contrast to about 40. ●

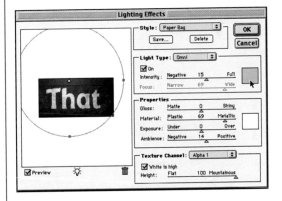

TOOLBOX

Duck Pattern

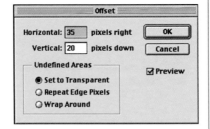

This technique demonstrates how to create patterns by duplicating layers and using the Offset filter. You can use the pattern to fill any selection, including—what do you know!—type selections.

1 Create a new file and create a new layer (Layer 1). Make the Background layer invisible. In the new layer, create a tile for the pattern. I used two of Photoshop 5.0's Assorted Brushes to create this tile. This tile is on the P5TM CD-ROM for you to use if you want. Open the file (P5TM➡P5TM files➡Patterns➡Duck Pattern), choose Select➡All, copy it, close the file, and paste in to Layer 1.

> **TIP** Making the Background layer invisible in Step 1 gives the pattern a transparent background. If you want the pattern to contain a background color, fill the Background layer with a color and keep it visible.

2 Duplicate Layer 1 and choose Filter➡Other➡Offset. Make sure that the Preview is turned on and set the Horizontal (35 pixels) and Vertical (20 pixels) values so that the copied tile moves down and to the right of the original. Make sure that the Vertical value is high enough to move the second tile down a distance equal to or greater than half the height of the tile.

3 From the Layers palette menu, choose Merge Down. Then duplicate the merged layer.

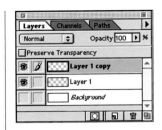

4 Press (Command-Option-F) [Control-Alt-F] to bring back the Offset filter dialog box. Set the Horizontal value to 0. Double the Vertical value.

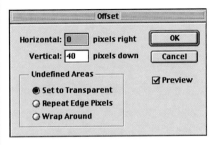

Watch the preview to make sure that the spacing looks good. Here's my design.

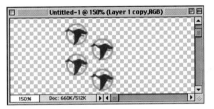

5 Double-click the Rectangular Marquee tool to select it and bring the Marquee Options palette to the front. On the palette, select the Fixed Size option and set the Width value to double the value used for the Horizontal Offset in Step 2. Set the Height to double the Vertical value used in Step 2.

6 Click the Marquee tool once in the image area to place the fixed selection. Drag the selection into place so that the horizontal dimension extends to the outside of the two columns of tile images. Vertically, the top of selection should start somewhere just below the center of the original tile image.

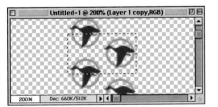

127

7 Choose Edit➡Define Pattern.
The pattern is now ready for use.
Delete all layers except the
Background layer. Deselect the
selection.

8 Choose a foreground color
(CMYK: 25, 0, 50, 0) for the tile
background, and use the Type tool
to enter the text (Berthold City at
130 points). Choose Layer➡Type➡
Render Layer.

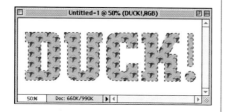

9 Load the transparency selection
of the type layer. Choose Edit➡Fill.
Select Pattern from the Use pop-up
menu (100%, Normal).

10 I added a stroke (Edit➡Stroke)
and a shadow (Layer➡Effects➡
Drop Shadow) to finish the effect.

VARIATIONS

Floating Patterns

Do Steps 1 through 8 to define a
pattern. If you want to use the pattern I used, open the Plane Pattern
file from the CD-ROM (P5TM➡
P5TM Files➡Patterns➡Plane
Patterns). Then choose Select➡All
and Edit➡Define Pattern before
closing the file. Create a new file
and do Step 8, then continue with
the rest of the Floating Pattern
steps.

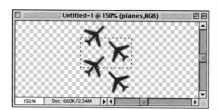

Before Step 9, create a new layer
(Layer 1). Complete Step 9.

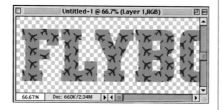

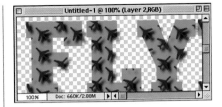

Photoshop's built-in Drop Shadow feature will not work here because the shadow needs to be contained within the type outlines. Create a new layer (Layer 2), move it beneath Layer 1, and load the transparency selection of Layer 1. Choose Select➡Feather (3 pixels) to soften the selection for the shadow. Choose a foreground color for the shadow (CMYK: 100, 100, 0, 60) and fill the selection. Then use the Move tool to nudge the shadow layer down and to the right.

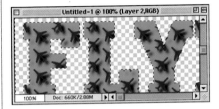

Load the transparency selection from the type layer, choose Select➡Inverse, and press Delete to get rid of the shadow areas that extended outside the borders of the type.

I added the stroke in Layer 1, but applied the drop shadow to the type layer.

Photoshop Patterns

There are a number of pattern tiles included with Photoshop 5.0. To use these patterns, open one of them (Photoshop 5.0➡Goodies➡ Brushes and Patterns➡Postscript Patterns). Choose Select➡All and Edit➡Define Pattern. Then do Steps 8 through 10. These files create seamless patterns. I opened the Weave-Y pattern…

…and used it to fill this type. ●

129

This is the only effect in the book that completely relies on a third-party plug-in—the KPT Page Curl 3.0 filter from MetaCreations. This technique will not work for all type, but it can be a nice addition in the right cases. Here are some guidelines for using this filter with type:

1 Create a new file and use the Type Mask tool to enter the text (Adobe Garamond Bold at 100 points). Choose a foreground color for the type (CMYK: 100, 0, 50, 0) and fill the selection. Then save the selection (Alpha 1).

2 Choose a background color to be placed beneath the upturned corners (CMYK: 0, 0, 100, 40). Choose the same color as the background if you don't want any color to appear below the corner.

TOOLBOX

KPT Page Curl 3.0

3 If the type is not already selected, load the Alpha 1 channel selection and then select the Rectangular Marquee tool. The filter does all the work for you in this effect, but you need to make the right selection to get the results that you want. Hold the (Option) [Alt] and Shift keys, and drag the Rectangular Marquee tool to make a selection that is as tall as you want the curl to be and includes the part of the letter that the curl will extend over. Make a selection like this. Holding the (Option) [Alt] and Shift keys inter-sects the new selection with the existing selection.

4 The top of the curl will be in the upper-right corner of the selection. Or depending on the selection that you make, in the imaginary top right corner—where the right most and uppermost edges of the selection meet. And the filter curls about one-fourth of the horizontal dimension of the selection.

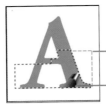
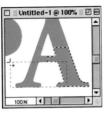

Imaginary top right corner

One-fourth of the horizontal dimension of the selection

5 Hold the Shift key and drag a rectangle to include any part of the area to the left of the curl that you want to include. Adding this selection gives the Page Curl filter somewhere to place the shadow cast by the curl. It also affects the horizontal dimension of the curl—the further this selection extends to the left, the further the curl will extend to the left.

6 Choose Filter➡KPT 3.0➡ KPTPage Curl 3.0. Press (Command-E) [Control-E] to change all the settings to their defaults. There are various settings that you can play with here, but I am going to stick to the basics.

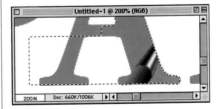

131

7 Press (Return) [Enter] to apply the filter.

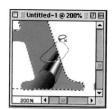

8 If you don't like the way that the curl lines up with the right edge of the letter, select the Lasso tool and hold the (Option) [Alt] and Shift keys while circling the area that you do not want to be part of the curl, like this:

9 Then fill the selection with the color of the type. With proper selecting, you can make the curl look like the shape of the serif.

10 Repeat Steps 3 through 9 to peel the corners of all the letters.

VARIATIONS

Darken
After Step 7, press (Command-F) [Control-F] to reapply the filter and make a darker curl and shadow.

Colorize
Load the Alpha 1 channel selection, and choose 50% gray for the foreground color. Choose Select➥ Color Range and use the Fuzziness slider to select as much of the curls as you can without selecting the type. A Fuzziness setting of 80 worked well for this example.

Choose Image➡Adjust➡Hue/Saturation, check the Colorize box, raise the Saturation to 100, and use the Hue slider to find a color.

Top Curls

The Page Curl filter enables you to make curls in any direction. Make a selection.

Then after changing the filter settings to their defaults in Step 6, click on one of the curls around the border of the preview to choose an alternate direction. ●

plaid

This effect works by combining four Photoshop filters (Fragment, Mosaic, Tile, and Facet) to make different plaids. I found that the following method works the best.

1 First, create a new file. Choose a foreground color for the color of the type, and then use the Type Mask tool to enter the text into a layer. I used 90-point Bauhaus type. Fill it with the foreground color.

2 Keep the selection active and choose Filter➡Stylize➡Tiles (Number of Tiles: 10; Maximum Offset: 1%). The Number of Tiles controls the number of vertical tiles that will be in your tallest letter. You can change the number of tiles, but keep the maximum offset at 1% so the grids lines are straight.

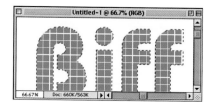

3 Now, go to the Channels palette, and click on one of the color channels to make it the only active channel. I made the Green channel the active channel. The tiled type looks gray because you are only viewing one color channel.

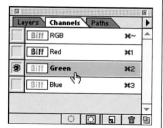

TIP You can choose any color channel. Each produces the same effect but displays different colors. You can also make two color channels active. The effect still works the same but again produces different colors.

4 Choose Filter➡Pixelate➡ Fragment. This filter divides the type into smaller segments. Because the information in all three color channels (Red, Green, and Blue) is mixed together to determine the colors that you see in the composite image, altering one of the color channels affects the color in the composite image. The Fragment filter does this by shifting the white areas (created by the Tiles filter) of only one of the channels (the Green channel in this case).

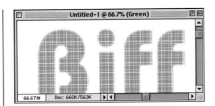

5 Now, for the magic. Press (Command-~) [Control-~] to return to the composite channel—instant plaid waits for you. Using the Fragment filter to shift the pixels of only one color channel produced new colors in the composite image.

6 To change the colors of the plaid, choose Image➡Adjust➡ Hue/Saturation and use the Hue slider to run through a closet full of plaids.

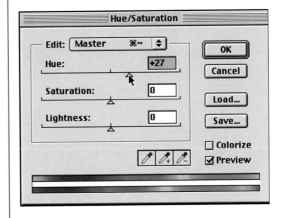

135

Here's the final type.

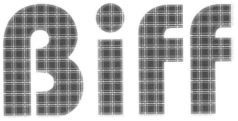

plaid

Muffy
Chip
Buffy
Theodore
Jock

VARIATIONS

The possibilities are endless. Here is a selection of plaids I made by applying just one more filter after completing Step 6:

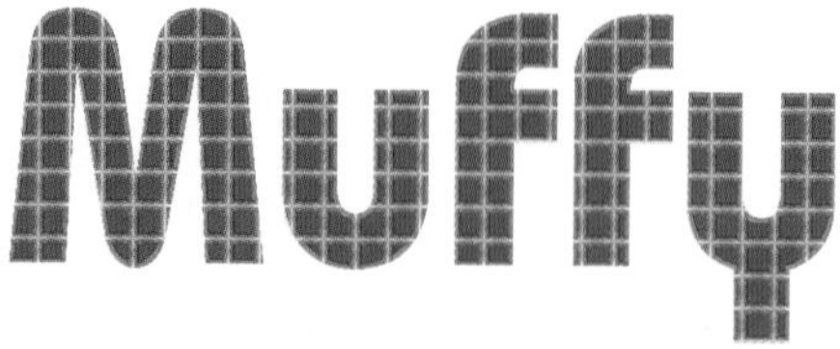

Select the Red channel and choose Filter➡Other➡Maximum (Radius: 2).

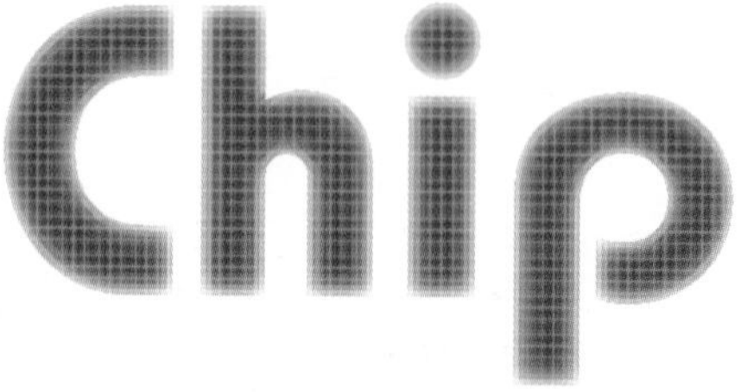

Or, try choosing Filter➡Pixelate➡Fragment. Keep applying the filter until the plaid glows.

Try Filter➡Pixelate➡Facet, and reapply the filter (Command-F) [Control-F] a few times.

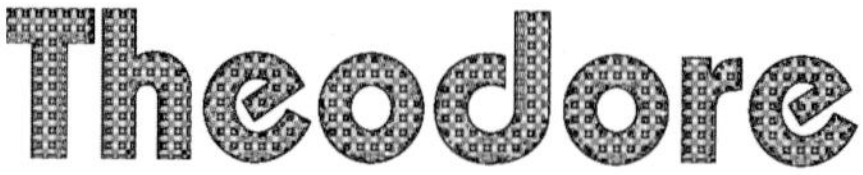

Here's what happens with Filter➡Stylize➡Find Edges applied several times.

Or choose only one color channel. (I chose the Green channel.) Choose Filter➡Stylize➡Find Edges, and apply the filter a second time (Command-F) [Control-F].

Add Some Texture

Keep the type selection active and choose Filter➡Render➡Lighting Effects. Use the settings shown here, or choose the Plaid preset from the Style pop-up menu. The most important setting is the texture channel. Choose one of the RGB channels. After you press OK, the plaid looks like it has some texture.

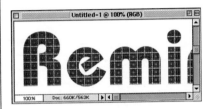

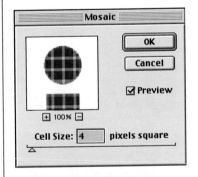

Monochrome Plaid

For a monochrome plaid with thick and thin cross lines, complete Steps 1 and 2; then choose Filter➡ Pixelate➡Mosaic. Watch the preview to find a Cell Size that gives you the desired effect. A Cell Size of 4 worked for me.

One More Road to Plaid

Complete Steps 1 through 3. Then choose Filter➡Pixelate➡Mosaic (Cell Size: 6). Return to the composite channel to see something like this. ●

PLUG-INS

Several software companies produce great plug-ins that you can add to Photoshop's Filter menu. This means that you, the type magician, can produce sophisticated effects by simply adjusting a few sliders. The following pages demonstrate the capabilities of some of the most popular and powerful plug-ins.

Eye Candy 3.0

There are 21 filters in this set from Alien Skin Software (http://www.alienskin.com), formerly known as the Black Box, ranging from shadows and glows to glass and fire. The interface contains a generous preview and all the controls to adjust almost every aspect of each effect. Here is the interface for the Glass filter.

And a few effects.

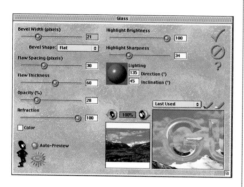

Inner Bevel

Glass

Fur

Fire

HotTEXT

This plug-in from Vertigo Technology (http://www.vertigo3d.com) is a fully featured 3D text machine. Not only can you create 3D text, but this plug-in enables you to also place the text on a path, choose lighting options, and map images onto the surface. It is powerful, but be forewarned that it will take some RAM to run it and some practice to master it. Here is the interface.

And a few examples.

Kai's Power Tools (KPT)

This set of plug-ins from MetaCreations (http://www.metatools.com) has been around for awhile for good reason. You can create an endless variety of textures and gradients through an interface that is intuitive and friendly. The Page Curl filter was already demonstrated in the Peel-Away effect. Besides the effects shown here, KPT 3.0 includes a number of filters for less exotic effects that improve the standard Photoshop tools. Here is the Texture Explorer interface...

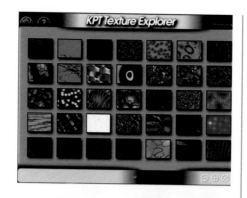

...and some of the effects from that and from other plug-ins in the set.

Texture Explorer

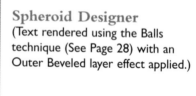

Gradient Designer

Spheroid Designer
(Text rendered using the Balls technique (See Page 28) with an Outer Beveled layer effect applied.)

Andromeda Series Filters

Six plug-in packages are available from Andromeda Software (http://www.andromeda.com). Each concentrates on a different aspect of image creation and manipulation. Series 1 contains a variety of imaging effects such as the Star filter that provides one more way to add highlights to your type.

The Techtures Filter (Series 4) does more than apply textures. It can map its library of textures to your type and contains other environment effects such as smoke and lightning. This set offers a great variety of textures. Here is the interface.

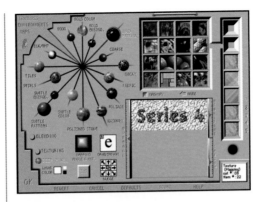

And here's a type image with a texture mapped to its surface.

The Andromeda Shadow Filter is a filter for—surprise!—creating shadows. It does a great job with casting perspective shadows because it enables you to control every aspect of the shadow. It even gradually increases the blur of the shadow as it recedes. ●

Use a displacement map to make the waves, the Lighting Effects filter to create the texture, and the Curves dialog box to add the shadows and you have a tasty midafternoon snack.

1 Open the Chipsmap.dis file from the P5TM CD (P5TM CD-ROM➡ P5TM Files➡Displacement Maps➡Chipsmap.dis).

2 Choose Select➡All, copy the image, and close the file.

3 Create a new RGB file, create a new channel (Alpha 1), and paste in the image. Deselect the selection.

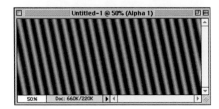

4 Return to the composite channel and set the foreground color to CMYK: 0, 0, 100, 40. Then use the Type tool to enter the text into a new layer (Futura Bold at 130 points). Choose Layer➡Type➡ Render Layer.

5 Choose Filter➡Distort➡ Displace (Horizontal Scale: 5%, Vertical Scale 5%, Stretch to Fit, Repeat Edge Pixels). Click OK.

TOOLBOX

Chipsmap.dis (displacement map)

Chips (Lighting Effects Style)

Another dialog box opens asking you to find a displacement map. Find P5TM CD-ROM➡P5TM Files➡Displacement Maps➡ Chipsmap.dis and click Open. This filter creates the waves around the edges of the type.

6 To add shadows to the ridges, load the selection from the Alpha I channel and choose Image➡Adjust➡Curves. Grab the center of the diagonal line in the grid and bend the curve upward about this far.

Click OK and deselect the selection to get this effect.

7 Create a new layer (Layer I) for the shadow and move the layer below the type layer.

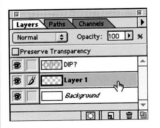

8 Load the transparency selection from the type layer; then subtract from that selection the selection from the Alpha I channel. Choose Select➡Feather (5 pixels). Set the foreground color to black and fill the selection to create a shadow that accentuates the ridges by varying the lights and darks.

143

9 Deselect the selection. Select the Move tool and nudge the shadow down and to the right by using the arrow keys. I pressed each key three times.

10 Load the transparency selection of the type layer and save it as a new channel (Alpha 2). Make the new channel (Alpha 2) the active channel.

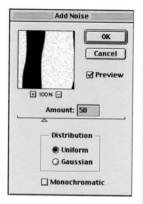

11 Choose Filter➞Noise➞Add Noise. Try these settings to add a small amount of noise that the Lighting Effects filter can use to create some texture on the surface of the chips (Amount: 35, Uniform).

12 Deselect the selection, return to the composite channel, and make the type layer the active layer. This is the layer that was created in Step 4 by the Type tool.

13 Choose Filter➞Render➞ Lighting Effects. Select the Chips preset style or match the settings seen here. Keep the texture amount low so this filter creates just a little roughness on the surface—not moon craters.

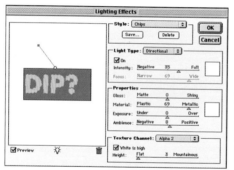

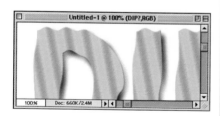

14 Finally, add a little noise to roughen the surface a little more. Choose Filter➥Noise➥Add Noise (Amount: 25, Uniform, Monochromatic).

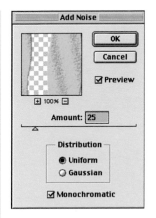

You can now create great embossed and beveled type with Photoshop 5.0's new layer effects features, and you can edit it! But if you want more dramatic raised type effects, try these techniques that use the Lighting Effects filter. For credit-cardlike type, see page ?? for an effect that modifies the built-in Emboss layer effect.

Plastic

1 Create a new file and choose a foreground color for the type (CMYK: 50, 0, 100, 0). Then use the Type tool to enter the text. I used Donata at 120 points. It will automatically be placed on a new layer. Choose Layer➡Type➡Render Layer.

2 Load the transparency selection of the new layer, create a new channel (Alpha 1), and fill the selection with white.

3 Keep the selection active and choose Filter➡Blur➡Gaussian Blur. The blur causes the type to be rounded when used as a texture channel with the Lighting Effects filter. The amount of blur affects the shape of the type. All you want is a little gray around the edges. Try 5 pixels.

146

TOOLBOX

Plastic (Lighting Effects Style)

License Plate (Lighting Effects Style)

4 Return to the composite channel and deselect the selection. Choose Filter➥Render➥Lighting Effects. This filter does the work. Select the Plastic preset style or match the settings seen in this figure. The texture channel should be the channel created in Step 2 (Alpha 1).

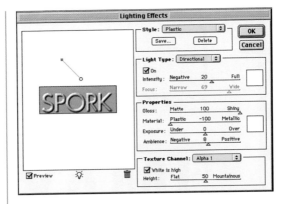

And the result.

 Pay attention to the settings in the Lighting Effects dialog box. This effect looks plastic because of the settings used. Vary the settings in the Properties box to adjust the character of the raised type.

License Plate

Here is a slight variation that has some fun with the basic Plastic technique.

1 Begin this effect on a white layer and use the Type Mask tool to enter the text (Helvetica Condensed Bold at 85 points). Save the selection as the Alpha 1 channel.

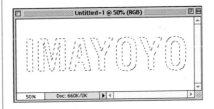

2 While the selection is still active, choose Select➥Modify➥Contract (1 pixel), Select➥Modify➥Smooth (2 pixels), and Select➥Feather (1 pixel). This softens the edges of the colored portion of the type.

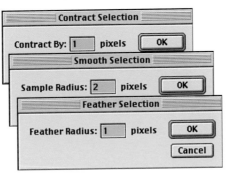

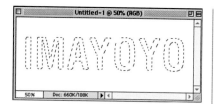

3 It seems like they never quite get the paint to sit directly on top of the raised metal letters. To replicate this effect, select the Marquee tool and use the arrow keys to nudge the selection slightly (two key-strokes to the left, and one key-stroke up).

4 Choose a foreground color for the type (CMYK: 0, 100, 100, 40) and fill the selection. Deselect the selection.

5 Make the Alpha 1 channel active. Choose Filter➡Blur➡Gaussian Blur and set the Gaussian Blur Radius to 3 pixels.

6 Then load the selection of the Alpha 1 channel (the same channel that is active). Press (Command-Option-F) [Control-Alt-F] to bring back the Gaussian Blur dialog box. Slide the Radius marker up until dark patches appear near the tips of the letters. I set the Radius at 9 pixels.

7 While the selection is still active, choose Image➡Adjust➡Invert to invert the type.

8 Then choose Image➡Adjust➡ Brightness/Contrast and slide the Brightness slider up until your type looks something like what you see in the figure. I raised the Brightness all the way to +100, chose Image➡ Adjust➡Brightness/Contrast again, and set the Brightness at +25. All this channel fuss produces a raised type that has a slight indentation in the center of the letters.

9 Return to the composite channel and deselect the selection. Choose Filter➡Render➡Lighting Effects. Use the License Plate preset style or match the settings in this figure.

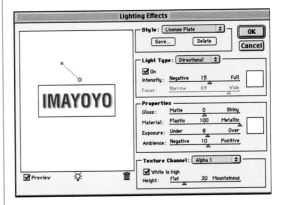

The final type.

Credit Card

1 Start this one with a background image for the credit card. I opened the 072 Plant image from the Photo 24 collection on the CD-ROM (P5TM➡Images➡Photo 24➡ Plants➡072), copied it, and pasted it into a new image file.

2 Choose a foreground color that is darker than the color you will use for the type (CMYK: 50, 0, 100, 40). Then use the Type tool to enter the text. The typeface is important for this one; OCR-B is a perfect credit card typeface. I set it at 36 points. Choose Layer➡ Type➡Render Layer.

149

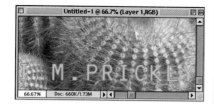

Untitled-1 @ 66.7% (Layer 1,RGB)

I.M.PRICKLY

66.67%   Doc: 660K/1.73M

I.M.PRICKLY

3 Create a new layer (Layer 1) and load the selection of the type layer. Choose Select➡Modify➡Contract. If your type is as small as mine, you can probably only contract the type 1 pixel before you start to lose the letters. Then choose Select➡ Feather (1 pixel). Choose a foreground color for the type and fill the selection.

4 Deselect the selection and make the original type layer the active layer. Choose Layer➡Effects➡Bevel and Emboss. Set the Style to Outer Bevel and raise the Depth all the way to 20 pixels.

TIP **If you link the two top layers together by making one of them active and clicking in the box to the left of the other on the Layers palette, you can move the raised type around the background and the bevel automatically adjusts to its new position.**

VARIATIONS

For slightly more complex highlights and shadows, complete the Plastic version on page 146 and then choose Layer➡Effects➡Bevel and Emboss. Select the Inner Bevel option and change the Shadow mode to Overlay (Angle: 120°, Depth: 10 pixels, Down, Blur: 5 pixels).

SPORK

The most crucial element of all the raised type effects is creating the channel used by the Lighting Effects filter as a texture map. Try this one.

In a new file, create a new channel (Alpha 1). Use the Type Mask tool to enter the text. I used Triplex at 150 points. Save the selection to create the Alpha 2 channel. Fill the selection with white and deselect the selection. Choose Filter➥ Blur➥Gaussian Blur (5 pixels), load the selection of the Alpha 1 channel, and press (Command-Option-F) [Control-Alt-F] to bring back the Gaussian Blur dialog box. Raise the Radius to approximately 25 pixels. Here is the channel.

Return to the composite channel, choose a foreground color for the type (CMYK: 0, 75, 100, 0), and fill the layer. Choose Filter➥Render➥ Lighting Effects (Plastic). Raise the Height to 100.

 To select only the type, load the selection of the Alpha 2 channel and choose Select➥Modify➥ Expand. Choose a value high enough to encompass the text (10 pixels) and choose Select➥Modify➥ Smooth. Set the Smooth value just enough so the selection is slightly rounded at the edges (3 pixels). ●

Untitled-1 @ 33.3

33.33%

Untitled-1 @ 66.7% (IOME,RGB)

66.67% Doc: 675K/1.28M

Layers Paths Channels

Normal Opacity: 100 %

Preserve Transparency

IOME

IOME copy

Background

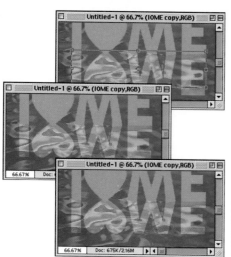

Untitled-1 @ 66.7% (IOME copy,RGB)

Untitled-1 @ 66.7% (IOME copy,RGB)

Untitled-1 @ 66.7% (IOME copy,RGB)

66.67% Doc:

66.67% Doc: 675K/2.16M

This effect is completed without the aid of channels. Instead, several layers are blended together to create a composite reflection.

1 Begin this effect with an image that contains a reflective surface such as this water image from the P5TM CD-ROM (P5TM CD-ROM➡Images➡D'Pix➡Ripples.JPG). The image was cropped and resized for this effect.

2 Choose a foreground color for the type (CMYK: 0, 50, 100, 0). Use the Type tool to enter the text (Triple Extra Bold at 100 points). It will automatically be placed on a new layer. Choose Layer➡Type➡Render Layer.

3 Duplicate the type layer and move the new layer below the type layer.

4 Choose Edit➡Transform➡Flip Vertical. Then use the Move tool to position the flipped type into place below the original type. Change the layer blending mode to Overlay.

5 Choose Edit➡Transform➡Scale, and hold the Shift key while dragging the bottom center tab upward. The objective is to compress the height of the reflection but don't go too far. Something like this would be great. Press Return to accept the transformation.

6 Choose Layer➡Add Layer Mask➡Reveal All. The layer mask will be used to fade the reflection into the water. Load the transparency selection of this layer.

7 Choose black for the foreground color and double-click on the Linear Gradient tool to select it and bring the Linear Gradient Options palette to the front. Select the Foreground to Transparent Gradient.

8 Drag the Gradient tool (while holding the Shift key) from the bottom of the reflected type to a point about two-thirds of the way up the height of the reflection. This fades the reflection into the water.

9 Drag the Gradient tool a second time from near the bottom of the original type to a short distance "below the surface." This second gradient helps the original type stand apart from the reflected type.

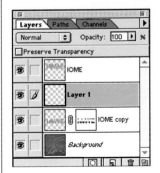

10 Create a new layer (Layer 1) and move it just below the original type layer. This layer holds a gradient that darkens the reflection near the surface of the water.

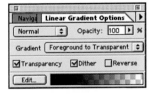

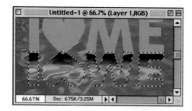

11 Keep the selection active, and select the Linear Gradient tool again. Keep the same settings chosen in Step 7. Drag the Gradient tool from a point near the bottom of the original type to a point about one-half of the way along the depth of the reflected type.

12 Change the layer Opacity to about 50%—and that's the basic reflection. The variations include a great addition to this effect.

VARIATIONS

Deselect any active selections, make the layer containing the water image active, and make all other layers invisible. Choose Select➡Color Range. Use the Eyedropper to select a highlight area of the water.

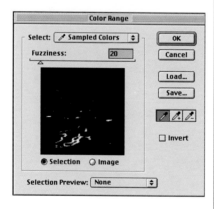

Then use the Fuzziness slider to control the selection so that only the lightest areas of the water are selected. The selected areas should be small.

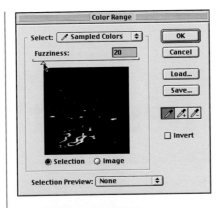

Make all layers visible and select the Lasso tool. Hold the (Option) [Alt] and Shift keys and circle an area of the water that includes all of the reflection and some of the surrounding water. There's no need to be precise. The purpose of the lassoing is to limit the selected areas.

Choose the same foreground color as you used for the type in Step 2. Fill the selection to add a few orange reflections to the surface of the water. If you have too much or too little orange, use the History palette to go back and reselect a new Color Range. Or if the orange is too strong, choose Filter➡Fade Fill and adjust the Opacity percentage to find the right strength. ●

155

Magic Brush

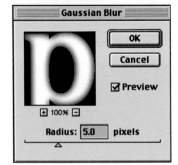

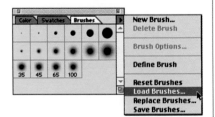

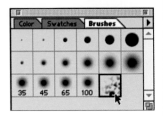

Here a custom paintbrush is used to create a texture for adding some 3D texture to the type.

1 Create a new file, choose a foreground color for your type (CMYK: 9, 75, 100, 40), and use the Type tool to enter the text (Weidemann at 95 points). Choose Layer➡ Type➡Render Layer.

2 Load the transparency selection of the type layer and save the selection as a new channel (Alpha 1). Make Alpha 1 the active channel.

3 Keep the selection active and choose Filter➡Blur➡Gaussian Blur. Set the Radius to approximately 5 pixels. The blur causes the type to raise when applying the Lighting Effects filter in Step 11. Deselect the selection.

4 Create a new channel (Alpha 2). Find the Brushes palette, choose Load Brushes from the palette menu, and load the Magic Brush file from the P5TM CD-ROM (P5TM CD-ROM➡P5TM Files➡Brushes➡ Magic Brushes).

5 One new brush appears as the last brush in the palette. Select the new brush, which was custom made by altering one of the brushes from Photoshop's Assorted Brushes collection.

6 Make the Alpha 1 channel visible so that you can see the type without altering it.

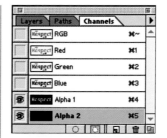

7 Make sure that the foreground color is white; select the Paintbrush tool and use it to drag two lines across the type (but in the empty Alpha 2 channel) like this.

8 Now to put the two channels together. Make Alpha 1 the active channel, make the Alpha 1 channel invisible, and load the selection from the Alpha 2 channel. Make sure the background color is black and press Delete to set the tracks into the type.

9 Return to the RGB channel and the Background layer. Load the selection of the Alpha 2 channel, set the foreground color to black and press (Option-Delete) [Alt-Backspace] to fill the tracks. Deselect the selection.

10 Choose Image➡Adjust➡Hue/ Saturation. Turn on the Colorize option, raise the Saturation and use the Hue slider to choose a color for the tracks. Here are the values I came up with: Hue: 32, Saturation: 50, Lightness: 0.

11 Make the type layer active and choose Filter➡Render➡Lighting Effects. Choose Trampled from the Style menu or match the settings you see here.

12 Depending upon the colors you have chosen, you might need to darken the areas where the tracks run over the letters. If so, create a new layer (Layer 1), load the transparency selection of the type layer, and then intersect that selection with the selection from the Alpha 2 channel. Ignore the warning message that will most likely pop up, and press (Option-Delete) [Alt-Backspace] to fill the selection with black. Change the layer blending mode to Overlay and lower the Opacity until the darkness is just right (50%).

13 Finally, I created some drop shadows and put everything together.

VARIATIONS

Now that you have the Magic Brush (Step 5), you can use it by itself to make tiretrack type. Just set the foreground color; then click and drag. ●

TOOLBOX

Scale Pattern

Scales (Lighting
Effects Style)

Magic Curves

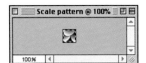

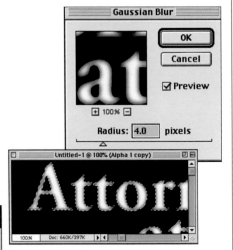

This effect shows you what you can do by combining techniques of texturing and patterning. A custom scales pattern is included on the P5TM CD-ROM for use with this effect.

1 Before beginning, open the Scale Pattern file from the CD-ROM (P5TM➡P5TM files➡Scales Pattern). Select All (Command-A) [Control-A], and choose Edit➡ Define Pattern. Close the file.

2 Open the file to contain the type and create a new channel (Alpha 1). Use the Type tool to enter the text. (I used Bodega Sans Black at 70 points.)

3 Duplicate the channel to create Alpha 1 copy. While the selection is still active, choose Filter➡Blur➡ Gaussian Blur. Use just enough to add a little gray around the edges. I set the Radius to 4.0 pixels.

4 The blur adds some roundness to the letters. Now you can use the Edit➡Fill command to blend the blur with the pattern defined in Step 1. Choose Edit➡Fill (Use: Pattern, Opacity: 100%, Mode: Multiply).

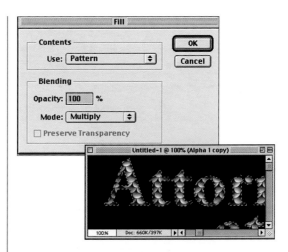

In the result, you can see that the edges of the pattern-filled type are slightly dark and a little blurry.

5 Return to the composite channel and create a new layer (Layer 1). The selection should remain active. Choose a foreground color and fill the type with the color. Here is the green that I used (CMYK: 75,0,100,0).

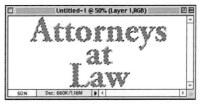

6 Choose Filter➡Render➡Lighting Effects. From the pop-up menu, choose Scales. (If it does not appear in the menu, you can match the settings that you see here, or flip to page 248 in the "What's on the CD-ROM" section to find out how to install the lighting effects that are on the CD.)

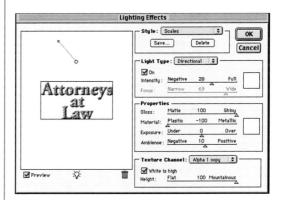

161

Attorneys
at
Law

Attorneys
at
Law

Click OK to see this new slimy type. Check out the variations for ideas on enhancing the scales.

VARIATIONS

Gloss
After completing Step 6 choose Filter➡Artistic➡Plastic Wrap. Try these settings: Highlight Strength: 15, Detail: 9, Smoothness: 15.

Small and Slick
If the scales' scaling doesn't quite fit your type, you can resize them. After opening the Scales Pattern file in Step 1, choose Image➡Image Size. In this example, I set the Width percentage to 50% to create smaller scales. If you make this file any smaller, the scales begin to lose their definition; try using larger type instead.

Image Size

Pixel Dimensions: 1K (was 1K)

Width: 50 [percent ▾]
Height: 11 [pixels ▾]

[OK]
[Cancel]
[Auto...]

Print Size:

Width: 0.077 [inches ▾]
Height: 0.073 [inches ▾]
Resolution: 150 [pixels/inch ▾]

☑ Constrain Proportions
☑ Resample Image: [Bicubic ▾]

Untitled-1 @ 50% (Layer 1,Alpha 1 copy 2)

What
Smells?

50%   Doc: 660K/1.50M

To create this slicker, less bumpy effect, finish the rest of the steps and then duplicate the Alpha 1 channel again to create Alpha 1 copy 2. The selection should still be active. Choose Filter➡Blur➡ Gaussian Blur. Raise the Radius slightly. I used 6 pixels.

Return to the composite channel and choose Filter➡Render➡ Lighting Effects. Select the Scale preset from the pop-up menu. Then change the Texture Channel to Alpha 1 copy 2.

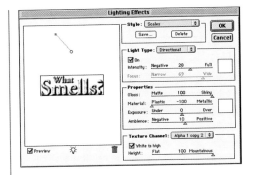

Kind of fishy.

What's That?

To create this texture, first use the resizing technique from Small and Slick to make the pattern 200% of its original size. Then, in Step 3, do not apply the Gaussian Blur. Instead of Step 4, choose Edit➡Fill (Use: Pattern, Opacity: 100%, Mode: Normal).

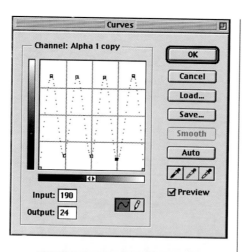

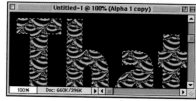

Then choose Image➜Adjust➜ Curves and either load the Magic Curves file from the CD (P5TM CD➜P5TM Files➜Magic Curves) or re-create the wave seen here. This wave radically alters the values in the channel. A wild pattern is produced that will be used by the Lighting Effects filter to make the texture you see in the final image.

In Step 5, fill the type selection with white. In Step 6, select the Scales preset; then change the exposure setting to -25 and Texture Height to 50.

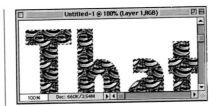

Finally, while the selection is still active, create a new layer (Layer 2) above Layer 1 and paste in a colorful image. Change the layer blending mode to Color. ●

Photoshop 5.0's new Drop Shadow Layer Effect is an excellent new feature that can take care of most of your shadow needs, but it takes the Transform feature to make this perspective shadow. The Transform feature and the Drop Shadow feature are used to make the floating shadows at the end of this chapter.

Perspective Shadows

I Create a new file and use the Type tool to enter the text (Utopia Black at 45 points). Then use the Move tool to position the text in the upper portion of the image window.

2 Load the transparency selection of the type layer and press Q to enter Quick Mask mode. Most of the shaping of the shadow will be done here. Choose Edit➡ Transform➡Flip Vertical and then use the Move tool to move the flipped type back up to meet the bottom edge of the original type.

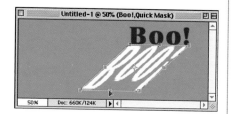

3 Choose Edit➡Free Transform. Hold the (Command) [Control] key and drag the bottom center handle of the transform box down and away from the original type. Holding the (Command) [Control] key enables you to move the bottom of the transform box from side to side, creating a parallelogram.

4 After slanting and stretching the flipped type, you can fine-tune the shadow by holding the (Command) [Control] key and adjusting the two bottom corner handles. Holding the (Command) [Control] key here enables you to move each handle independently. Watch out for the top of the shadow where it meets the bottom of the type. The distorted shadow type will have a tendency to shift to one side of the original type. Don't move these handles too much.

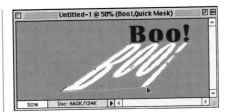

5 Press (Return) [Enter] to accept the changes. Then double-click the Linear Gradient tool to select it and bring the Linear Gradient Options palette to the front. Set the Gradient to Foreground to Transparent (Normal, Opacity: 100%) and make sure that the foreground color is black.

6 Click and drag the Linear Gradient tool upward from the bottom of the shadow. Hold the Shift key as you drag to keep the gradient perfectly straight.

7 Choose Filter➥Blur➥Gaussian Blur. Blur the Quick Mask just enough to take the hardness off the edges of the shadow. I set the Radius to 1 pixel.

8 Press Q to exit Quick Mask mode. Choose a foreground color for the shadow (I used black), make the Background layer the active layer and fill the shadow selection. Deselect the selection.

Floating Shadows

After entering the type, choose Layer➡Type➡Render Layer. Then choose Edit➡Free Transform. Press (Command-Shift-Option) [Control-Shift-Alt] and grab one of the top corner tabs. Drag the corner toward the center of the text. Press (Return) [Enter] to accept the changes. Finally, choose Layer➡Effects➡Drop Shadow. The key to making the type looking like it floats is a high Distance setting—60 pixels in this example.

This alternate floating shadow was started by choosing Layer➡ Effects➡Drop Shadow to create a drop shadow. Then choose Layer➡Effects➡Create Layer. A new layer is created that contains the drop shadow. Make the Drop Shadow layer the active layer, and choose Edit➡Free Transform. Click in the center of the transform box to move the shadow down and away from the type. Grab the top center tab, hold the Shift key, and compress the shadow almost completely—until the top and bottom tabs are stacked directly on top of each other. Press (Return) [Enter] to accept the changes. Choose Filter➡Blur➡Motion Blur (Angle: 0°, Distance: 20 pixels) and then Filter➡Blur➡Gaussian Blur (2 pixels). ●

Boo Hoo

ShatterMap
(displacement
map)

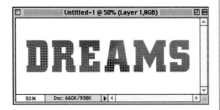

In this technique, the Displace filter is used to break the type apart and scatter the shards. There is a custom displacement map on the CD-ROM that can be loaded and resized to fit your type.

1 You can shatter anything with this type, including type created by other techniques in this book. To do this make sure that the type image is flattened into a single layer and make that layer active. This type was created with the Reflector technique on page 46. Or use the Type tool to enter the text.

2 Open the ShatterMap file from the P5TM CD-ROM (P5TM➡P5TM Files➡Displacement Maps➡ShatterMap).

3 Choose Select➡All and copy the image. Close the file and return to the type image. Create a new channel (Alpha 1) and paste in the ShatterMap image. Make the composite channel visible and keep the selection active.

4 Choose Edit➡Transform➡Scale. Scale the ShatterMap so that it covers all the type. You can see in this view where the type will be shattered. Resizing this image will allow the shattering that takes place in Steps 7 and 8 to align with the selections that are made in Steps 9 and 10.

5 Deselect the selection, make the composite channel invisible, and choose Duplicate channel from the Channels palette menu. Set the Destination to New and name the file (DreamShat). Click OK. When the new file opens, save it (Photoshop format) and close it.

6 Next, duplicate the Alpha 1 channel and make the new channel (Alpha 1 copy) active. Choose Filter➡Stylize➡Find Edges and Image➡Adjust➡Invert. The Find Edges filter turns the ShatterMap into a web of sharp lines.

7 Return to the composite channel, and choose Filter➡Distort➡Displace. Set the Horizontal and Vertical Scale percentages to 7 (Stretch to Fit, Wrap Around). Click OK.

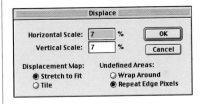

171

8 A dialog box appears asking you to find a Displacement Map. Find the file that you saved in Step 4 (DreamShat). The Displace filter shifts areas of the original image (the type in this case) according to the values in the chosen displacement map.

TIP If the Displace filter distorted the type too much, go back to Step 6 (by using the History palette) and use lower settings for the Scale percentages.

9 Load the selection of the Alpha 1 channel. Then choose Image➡Adjust➡Brightness/Contrast. Raise both the Brightness (+80) and Contrast (+30) so the individual shards of type are distinguishable.

10 Next, load the selection of the
Alpha 1 copy channel and press
Delete. This separates the shards by
clearing thin lines between them.
Deselect the selection.

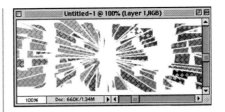

11 To define the edges, choose a
foreground color to use as a stroke
color (CMYK: 100, 75, 0, 40). Then
load the transparency selection
of the type layer, and choose Edit➡
Stroke (1 pixel, 100%, Normal,
Outside). I also used the Drop
Shadow layer effect to finish off
the type. ●

There are numerous methods in Photoshop to create multicolored textures. Here is one that gives great results, using the Radial Gradient tool and the Glass filter.

1 Create a new layer (Layer 1) and use the Type tool to enter the text. (I used Copperplate Bold at 100 points.) Choose Layer➡Type➡Render Layer. Turn on the Preserve Transparency option for the type layer. This causes the gradients to stay within the boundaries of the type when you use the Gradient tool in Step 3.

2 Choose Layer➡Effects➡Bevel and Emboss. This colored texture looks great on raised type. Select the Inner Bevel style (Depth: 20, Blur: 10).

3 Double-click on the Radial Gradient tool to select it and bring the Radial Gradient Options palette to the front. Select a gradient from the list (or create one of your own) that has at least four colors in it. If you're not creating your own, the presets limit you to the Yellow, Violet, Orange, Blue gradient— which is what I chose. Don't be too concerned with the colors in the gradient. They affect the final colors, but we are going to alter them anyway. The surprises this effect produces are part of the magic.

4 Click the Edit button to open the Gradient Editor; then click the Transparency radio button. You see a black bar with one slider at each end. At the bottom of the dialog box is a preview of the gradient. Click once below the bar to create a new slider. Move it to the 95% Location.

5 Then click on the far right slider and change the Opacity to 0%. Click OK to confirm the changes you made.

6 Now use the Radial Gradient tool to click and drag many gradients across the type. Making many small gradients helps to break up the colors. Here is the type covered with gradients. The colors stays inside the type outlines and your type remains beveled. Make sure to cover all the type with gradients—don't leave any of the original type color (black) showing.

7 The Clouds and Difference Clouds filters use the foreground and background colors to create their clouds. You will not see these colors when using the Difference Clouds filter in this step, but they do matter. For the purposes of this technique, it is important to know that the difference between the colors affects the final type. Choosing two colors far apart produces the greatest variety of colors and choosing colors near to each other produces the smallest variety of colors. I pressed D to set the colors at their defaults (black and white). After selecting colors, choose Filter➡Render➡Difference Clouds.

8 Then select Image➡Adjust➡ Invert. After applying the Difference Clouds filter, the colors turned dark. Because I wanted brighter colors I inverted them. This step is optional.

9 Choose Image➡Adjust➡Levels. Now, there is too much white. Grab the black Input slider and move it to the right to increase the amount of dark colors. I also nudged the gray slider slightly to the right.

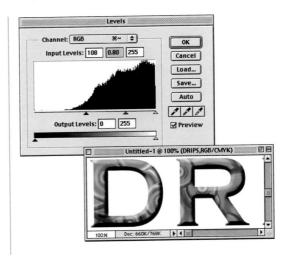

10 Choose Image➡Adjust➡ Hue/Saturation. Raising the Saturation (+100) sharpens the contrast between bordering colors and makes all the colors brighter at the same time. You can also take this opportunity to use the Hue slider to choose a different set of colors.

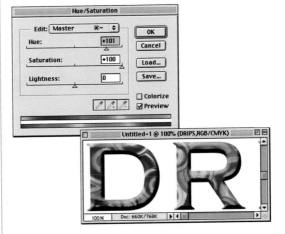

177

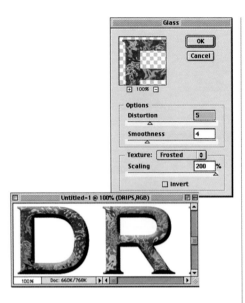

Glass

OK
Cancel

100%

Options
Distortion   5
Smoothness   4

Texture: Frosted
Scaling   200 %

Invert

Untitled-1 @ 100% (DRIPS,RGB)

DR

100%   Doc: 660K/768K

DRIPS

11 Finally, the Glass filter produces the texture. This filter reveals a background color in some areas when it distorts the colors. Choose a background color that fits into the color scheme already in the type. I chose a blue color (CMYK: 100, 50, 0, 0). Then choose Filter➡Distort➡Glass. Set the Distortion to 5, the Smoothness to 4, the Texture to Frosted, and the Scaling to 200%.

12 I added a drop shadow to the final image.

VARIATIONS

After Step 12, apply Filter➡
Sharpen➡Sharpen More five times.

Monochrome

This technique can also create a
nice monochromatic texture. After
completing all of the previous
Steps, choose Image➡Adjust➡
Hue/Saturation. Click on the
Colorize option, raise the
Saturation, and use the Hue slider
to find a color. I also chose
Image➡Adjust➡Auto Levels for a
better distribution of darks and
lights.

Texture

Apply these two filters after Step
11 for another texture:
Filter➡Pixelate➡Fragment and
Filter➡Artistic➡Paint Daubs
(Brush Size: 9, Sharpness: 24, Brush
Type: Simple). ●

This colored glass effect breaks the type into small pieces and adds distortion, color, and some lead trim. The variations provide some useful adjustments to the basic effect.

1 Open the file that contains the background image that you want to place the stained glass type on top of. I opened this file from the P5TM CD-ROM (P5TM➡Images➡Photo 24➡Plants➡024).

2 Choose 50% gray for the foreground color and use the Type tool to enter the text (Humanist 521 Extra Bold Condensed at 130 points). Be sure to use a heavy typeface that has plenty of room for dividing the interior into the smaller shapes seen in the thumbtab image.

3 Load the transparency selection of the new layer and save the selection to create the Alpha 1 channel. Choose Layer➡Type➡Render Layer. Make the Background layer invisible so you can see only the type.

180

TOOLBOX

Magic Curves

4 While the selection is still active, choose Filter➡Noise➡Add Noise (Amount: 50, Gaussian, Mono-chromatic). The Amount is not very critical as long as there is enough noise that you can see it easily.

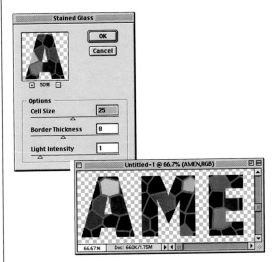

5 Choose a bright color for the foreground color. (I used CMYK: 0, 100, 100, 0.) The Stained Glass filter will divide the type into pieces, using this color to separate the shapes. Using a bright color will make it easy to select the borders in Step 6. Deselect the selection, and choose Filter➡Texture➡ Stained Glass (Cell Size: 25, Border Thickness: 8, Light Intensity: 1). The Cell Size determines the size of the panes of glass within the letters and the Border Thickness determines the thickness of the lead that runs between the glass panes.

6 Choose Select➡Color Range. Because the foreground color is still the same bright color selected in Step 4, the Color Range auto-matically selects that color from the image. If necessary, adjust the Fuzziness slider so that all of the red is selected. Click OK to make the selection.

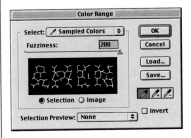

181

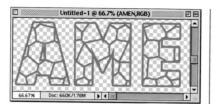

7 Choose Select➥Inverse and press Delete. Only the red borders should remain. Load the selection of the Alpha 1 channel; then choose Select➥Modify➥Expand (6 pixels). The Expand amount determines the thickness of the lead that runs around the perimeter of the letters. Subtract the selection of the Alpha 1 channel from the current selection. A thin border should now be selected around the perimeter of the letters. Fill the selection and deselect the selection.

8 Choose 50% gray for the foreground color again, turn on the Preserve Transparency option for the current layer, and fill the layer.

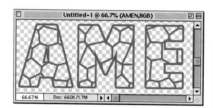

9 Choose Layer➥Effects➥Bevel and Emboss. Choose the Inner Bevel Style, set the Angle as you want (120°, Up), the Depth to 5 pixels, and the Blur to 3 pixels. Set the Highlight Mode to Color Dodge (Opacity: 75%) and the Shadow Mode to Color Burn (Opacity: 75%).

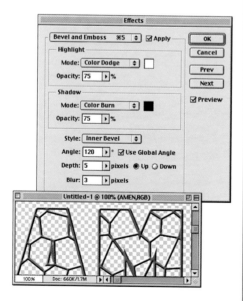

10 Load the transparency selection of the current layer; choose Select➡Inverse and intersect the selection with the selection of the Alpha 1 channel. All of the transparent areas within the type should now be selected. Save the selection to create the Alpha 2 channel and make the Alpha 2 channel the active channel.

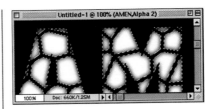

11 Keep the selection active and choose Filter➡Blur➡Gaussian Blur (5 pixels). Blur the selection enough to add some good gray edges to the interior of the shapes.

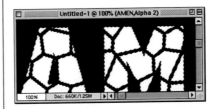

12 Duplicate the Alpha 2 channel to create the Alpha 3 channel. Then choose Image➡Adjust➡Curves and click the Load button. Find the Magic Curves file on the P5TM CD-ROM (P5TM➡P5TM Files➡ Miscellaneous➡Magic Curves) or draw the curve that you see in this figure.

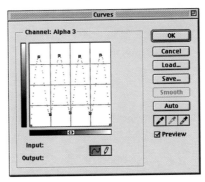

Click OK to accept the changes. Deselect the selection.

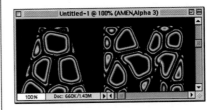

183

13 Make the Alpha 2 channel the active channel again. Choose Duplicate Channel from the Channels palette menu. Select New for the Destination Document and name the new document (StainTex).

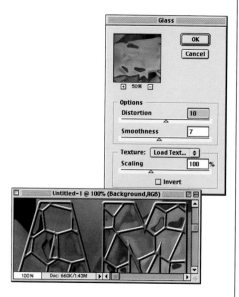

14 A new image window opens. Save the file (Photoshop format) and close it.

15 Return to the composite channel, and make the Background layer active. Choose Filter➡Distort➡Glass. Select the Load Texture option from the Texture menu. Find the StainTex file that was saved in Step 13 and open it. Adjust the settings to increase or decrease the amount of the distortion.

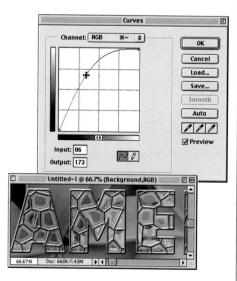

16 Load the selection of the Alpha 3 channel and choose Image➡Adjust➡Curves. Grab the line on the graph and bend the line up toward the upper-left corner to lighten the selected areas.

17 Deselect the selection, create a new layer (Layer 1), and set the layer blending mode to Color (75% Opacity).

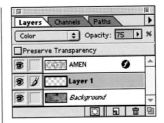

18 Make the layer containing the lead border the active layer. Double-click the Magic Wand tool to select it and bring the Magic Wand options palette to the front. Set the Tolerance to 1. You can now use the Magic Wand tool to select the individual areas within the lead borders. Click once with the Magic Wand inside one of the transparent areas.

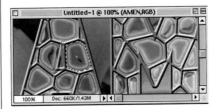

19 Make Layer 1 the active layer, and choose a foreground color for the piece of glass (CMYK: 100, 0, 100, 40). Dark colors will work best. Fill the selection to color it.

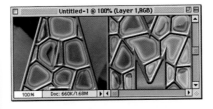

20 Keep repeating Steps 17 and 18 to fill all of the pieces within the letters. Make sure that you switch back and forth between the layer containing the lead and the color layer. (You don't need to double-click the Magic Wand tool and set the Tolerance each time you repeat the steps.)

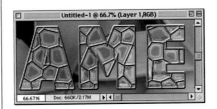

21 Make the lead layer the active layer and choose Filter➡Noise➡ Add Noise (20, Uniform, Mono-chromatic) to add some texture to the lead.

VARIATIONS

Lead Adjustments

To make the lead and glass panes appear like they are on the same level, double-click on the "f" that appears in the Layers palette next to the text layer name. Choose Bevel and Emboss from the pop-up menu and change the Angle to -60°, Down. Then choose Drop Shadow from the pop-up menu and click on the Apply box. Try these settings to add a small shadow to the glass panes: Angle: -60°, Distance: 3 pix-els, Blur: 3 pixels.

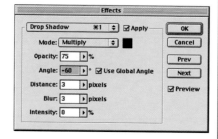

Raised Glass

To make the glass panes pop up from the lead, use the previous variation with these changes: Inner Bevel Angle: 120°, Down; Drop Shadow Angle: 120°.

No background

To get rid of the background around the type, load the selection of the Alpha 1 channel and choose Select➡Modify➡Expand. Expand the selection the same amount as in Step 7. Choose Select➡Inverse, make the Background layer the active layer, and fill the selection with white.

Jewels

Make these two changes to make a studded jewel effect. In Step 5, set the Border Thickness in the Stained Glass filter to 16. Then in Step 7, expand the selection by 12 pixels. Finish the rest of the steps. ●

This technique shows you how to make type stamps that you can use to build words or fill type outlines.

1 Create a new file and set the foreground color to black (which will ensure the hardness of the type when used as a brush). Use the Type tool to enter the text. Use a small point size. The type that was used here is Love Letter Typewriter at 10 points. Choose Layer➡Type➡ Render Layer.

TIP When using small point sizes, you might prefer to turn off the antialiasing option in the Type dialog box. If you don't, the type might be blurred. Make the same adjustment in the Brush Options dialog box in Step 4.

2 Zoom in on the type. Then select the Marquee tool and drag a rectangular selection around the type.

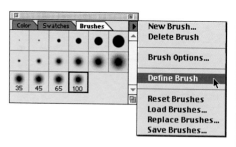

3 Double-click the Paintbrush tool to select it. Then find the Brushes palette, and choose Define Brush from the palette menu.

4 If you clicked and dragged the word, now all the letters would blur together and the stamped word would be illegible. To fix that problem, double-click the brush you created (on the Brushes floating palette).

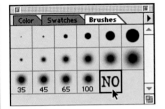

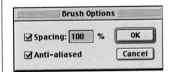

A dialog box appears that will enable you to change the Brush Spacing. The Spacing is the distance the brush will move, relative to the vertical height of the brush (the text), before placing another stamp. Change the Spacing to 100%.

5 The selection should still be active. Press Delete to clear it and deselect the selection. Double-click the Zoom tool to return to 100% view; then set the foreground color to a color for the stamp (CMYK: 0, 75, 100, 0), and simply "paint" the type.

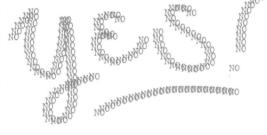

| TIP | Another useful setting on the Paintbrush Options palette is the Fade amount. Type a number in the Fade box (I used 120 for the "yes" and 10 for the exclamation mark), and set the "Fade to" to Transparent. The type will now fade away as you drag the stamp. |

189

VARIATIONS

1 Try using the stamp with a image. Open a file that has an image in it. These apples were clipped from a sample image packaged with Adobe Photoshop 4 (Adobe Photoshop 4➡Samples➡Fruit).

2 Create a new layer (Layer 2). Change the layer blending mode to Color Dodge, and paint the type over the photo.

For the second apple, I created a new layer (Layer 3) and set the layer blending mode to Color Burn.

For this variation, I painted with a stamp inside a type selection. Here is the stamp I used.

Next, use the Type Mask tool to enter the text (Compacta at 150 points).

Change the foreground color to a color for the type. Select the Paintbrush tool again, and paint into the selection.

If you feather the selection above by choosing Select→Feather (5 pixels) before you paint in the text, you will get something like this.

Try making other brushes for painting type. I painted a paw, defined it as a brush, changed its spacing to 105%, and then painted this text.

Try using one of the built-in brushes in Photoshop. From the Brushes floating palette arrow menu, choose Load Brushes. Find the Assorted Brushes file on your hard disk: Adobe Photoshop 5.0➡Goodies➡ Brushes & Patterns➡Assorted Brushes. Open this file. You can use any of these brushes to paint your type. Don't forget that you can adjust the spacing for any of these brushes.

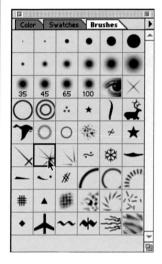

I made this image with the brush that was selected in the previous figure.

Stones (Lighting
Effects Style)

The Stained Glass filter starts the
Stones effect by dividing up the letters. From there, a little selection
manipulation takes you to the
Lighting Effects filter, which rounds
out the stones and the effect.

1 Create a new file. Use the Type
tool to enter the text. I used a
thick font named Cooper Black at
80 points. The type will be placed
automatically on a new layer.
Choose Layer➡Type➡Render
Layer.

2 Choose white for the foreground
color. Then choose Filter➡
Texture➡Stained Glass. Watch the
preview to see the approximate
sizes of the stones. Adjust the
Border Thickness slider for spacing
between the stones, and set the
Light Intensity to 0. These settings…

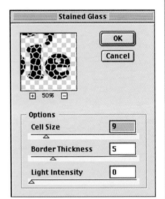

…will yield this picture:

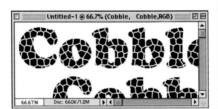

3 Select the Magic Wand tool and
click the wand inside one of the
black spots.

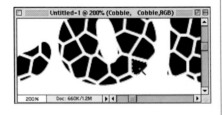

4 Choose Select➥Similar. Save this selection to create the Alpha 1 channel. Then choose Select➥ Modify➥Smooth. Smooth the selection approximately 3 pixels.

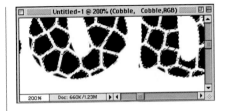

5 Choose Layer➥New➥Layer Via Copy to float the smoothed selection into a new layer (Layer 1). Make the original type layer invisible.

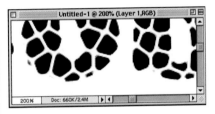

6 Turn on the Preserve Transparency option for Layer 1 on the Layers floating palette. Change the foreground color to black, and press the (Option-Delete) [Alt-Delete] keys to fill the layer with black. Then turn off the Preserve Transparency option. A few stones still might be attached to each other.

7 To get rid of these connections, load the Alpha 1 channel selection. Choose Select➥Inverse and press Delete. Deselect the selection.

193

8 Next, duplicate Layer 1 to create Layer 1 copy. Then make Layer 1 the active layer again.

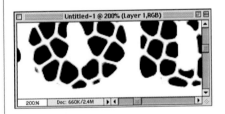

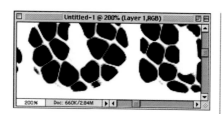

9 Select the Move tool and use the arrow keys to move this layer, which will be the shadow. I moved it two keystrokes to the right and two keystrokes down. It looks like the type is spreading in the direction you move it.

10 Then load the transparency selection for Layer 1 copy. Press Delete. You shouldn't see anything change, except for traces of white around the lower right of the stones.

11 Deselect the selection, and choose Filter➧Blur➧Guassian Blur. Blur the shadow just a little, about 1 pixel. The lightness of the shadow near the edge of the stones makes this homemade shadow work out better for this effect than Photoshop's built-in drop shadow feature.

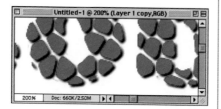

12 Make Layer 1 copy active and load the transparency selection for this layer. Choose 40% gray for the foreground color and fill the selection.

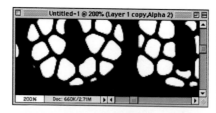

13 Save the selection to create the Alpha 2 channel. Make the Alpha 2 channel active.

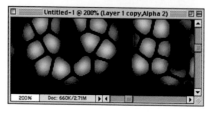

14 While the selection is still active, choose Filter➧Blur➧ Gaussian Blur. Raise the radius to about 4.5 pixels. Because the selection is active, blurring appears only inside the white areas.

15 Return to the composite channel, and make Layer 1 copy the active layer.

16 Next, choose Filter➡Render➡ Lighting Effects. You can select the Stones preset from the pop-up menu or match these settings (which are very similar to the Default settings). Move the light in the Preview box if necessary.

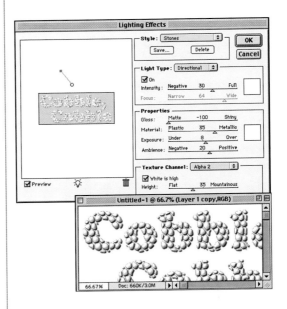

17 For the final touch, choose Filter➡Noise➡Add Noise. Adjust the Amount to your liking. I set it at 25, and turned on the Gaussian option. Turn the Monochromatic option on as well. ●

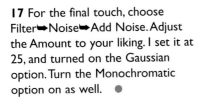

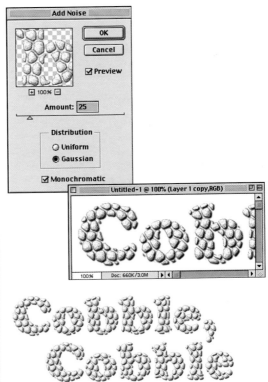

In this technique, the Displace and Lighting Effects filters are used in tandem to create type that appears to be mapped onto an irregular surface. You can create your own surfaces or use the ones that I have created. First I'll show you the method; then I'll show you some of the ways you can use it.

1 Creating surface maps is done in a channel. The best strategy is to fill the channel with a pattern and then use various filters to manipulate the pattern. To produce the first example here, open the Circle Pattern file from the P5TM CD-ROM (P5TM➡P5TM Files➡Patterns➡ Circle Pattern). Choose Select➡All and Edit➡Define Pattern. Close the file.

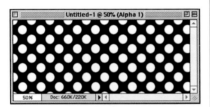

2 In a new file, create a new channel (Alpha 1) and choose Edit➡Fill (Use: Pattern, 100%, Normal).

TOOLBOX

Circle Pattern

Circle Pattern Small

Surface (Lighting Effects Style)

3 Duplicate the channel to make the Alpha 2 channel. Load the selection of the Alpha 1 channel; choose Select➡Inverse and Filter➡Blur➡Gaussian Blur. Blur the selection just enough to bring out some gray around the edges of the circles (8 pixels).

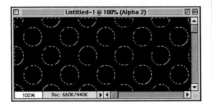

4 Choose Select➡Inverse again and choose Image➡Adjust➡Invert.

5 Deselect the selection and bring back the Gaussian Blur filter dialog box (Command-Option-F) [Control-Option-F]. Lower the Blur Radius to approximately 3 pixels. This channel will be the surface map for the type.

6 Choose Duplicate Channel from the Channels palette menu, select New from the Document menu, and name the file (Blurred Circles). When the new file opens, save it (Photoshop format) and close it.

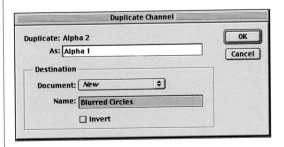

7 Return to the composite channel, choose a foreground color for the type (CMYK: 54, 0, 72, 0), and use the Type tool to enter the text. I used Kabel Ultra at 85 points. Choose Layer➡Type➡Render Layer.

8 Choose Select➡All and choose Filter➡Distort➡Displace. Set the Horizontal and Vertical values low and equal to each other. I set them both at 5%. It is important to select the entire layer before using the Displace filter. Otherwise the distorted shape of the type will not align with the highlights and shadows created by the Lighting Effects filter.

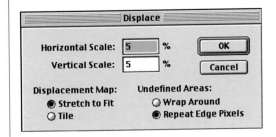

9 Click OK and a dialog box opens asking you to find a displacement map to use. Find the file that you saved in Step 6 (Blurred Circles), and click Open. The edges of the type will react to the distortion, but there should not be any changes inside the type.

197

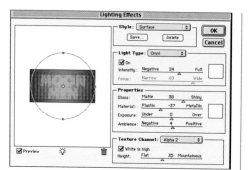

10 The type has been shaped. To add the highlights and shadows, choose Filter➥Render➥Lighting Effects. Either select the Surface preset or match the settings seen here. The texture map should be the channel that was duplicated in Step 6 (Alpha 2), and the Height should be kept low.

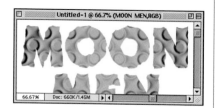

The distortions made by the Displace filter and the highlights and shadows created by the Lighting Effects filter should appear to fit each other.

11 Adding a drop shadow enhances the three-dimensional nature of this effect. Use the built-in drop shadow feature (Layer➥Effects➥Drop Shadow) with the default settings.

VARIATIONS

Holy Perforated Surfaces!

For this variation, I opened the Circle Pattern Small file in Step 1 (P5TM➥P5TM Files➥Patterns➥ Circle Pattern Small). This file is identical to the Circle pattern file but it has been compressed into a smaller size. Repeat Steps 1 through 5. Here is what the Alpha 1 copy channel looks like after Step 5.

Repeat Steps 6 through 10 (Kabel at 82 points; CMYK: 0, 54, 72, 0).

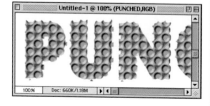

Then load the selection of the Alpha 1 channel and press Delete. Then follow Step 11 to create something like this.

Photoshop PostScript Patterns

There are a number of patterns included with Photoshop 5.0. You can use these patterns with this technique.

In Step 1, open the Herringbone 2 file (Photoshop 5.0➡Goodies➡ Brushes & Patterns➡PostScript Patterns➡Herringbone 2). Choose Image➡Adjust➡Invert; then Select➡All and Edit➡Define Pattern. Close the file but don't save the changes.

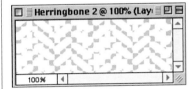

Follow Step 2; then load the selection of the Alpha 1 copy channel. Choose Filter➡Blur➡Gaussian Blur and set the Radius so that the white areas begin to look rounded (2.5 pixels). Then deselect the selection and choose Filter➡Blur➡ Gaussian Blur again. Lower the Radius to about 1 pixel. That completes the texture channel.

Complete the rest of the steps.

199

To make this a two-color image, load the selection from the Alpha 1 channel; then choose Image➡ Adjust➡Hue/Saturation. Use the Hue slider to find a second color and use the Saturation and Lightness sliders for fine-tuning.

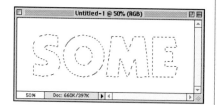

Type on Type

The last variation maps type across words raised from the background.

Choose a foreground color for the type (CMYK: 0, 100, 75, 25) and use the Type Mask tool to enter the text (Kabel Ultra at 115 points). This type will be the colored type that is mapped onto the textured type.

If you want to rotate the type as I have done here, choose Select➡ Transform Selection and use the handles to manipulate the type. When satisfied, press (Return) [Enter] and fill the selection with the foreground color. Deselect the selection.

Create a new channel (Alpha 1) and use the Type Mask tool to enter the text (Kabel Ultra at 115 points). Again choose Select➡Transform Selection if you want to rotate the type. Fill the selection with white.

Keep the selection active and choose Filter➡Blur➡Gaussian Blur. Adjust the Radius so that type begins to look rounded. I set it at 8 pixels.

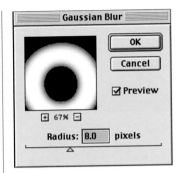

Perform Step 6, return to the composite channel, and then complete Steps 8 through 10. In Step 8, I set the Displace percentages both to 3%. ●

Torn (Lighting
Effects Style)

It's time to get in touch with your peelings. Create stripes using paths and the Stroke Subpath command. Then use the Lighting Effects filter to set them apart from each other.

1 Choose a foreground color for the type (CMYK: 20, 100, 100, 0) and use the Type tool to enter the text. I used Meta Plus Black at 90 points. Choose Layer➡Type➡ Render Layer.

2 Open the Brushes palette and double-click on any round brush to open the Brush Options dialog box. The Diameter determines the width of the stripes running through the type. I set it at 35 pixels. (Hardness: 100%, Spacing: 25%, Angle: 0°, Roundness: 100%).

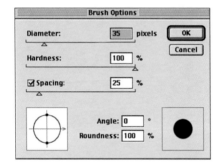

3 Create a new channel (Alpha 1), and make the RGB channels visible. You should see the type created in Step 1 appear within a red haze. The red haze lets you know that more than one channel is visible, but don't worry—the channel that is highlighted in the channels palette (Alpha 1) is the only channel that will be affected.

4 Select the Freeform Pen tool and drag it across the type to create a new path.

5 Make sure that the Foreground color is white, and double-click on the Paintbrush tool to bring the Paintbrush Options palette to the front. Choose Reset Tool from the palette menu. This sets up the Paintbrush for use by the Stroke SubPath command. Find the Paths palette and click on the Stroke SubPath icon at the bottom of the palette.

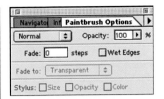

Choose Turn Off Path from the Path palette menu. You should now have a stripe through the type.

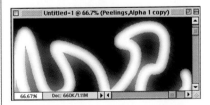

TIP It makes no difference whether or not you make one path or many paths. To make more than one path, simply keep repeating Steps 4 and 5.

6 Duplicate the channel to create Alpha I copy. Load the selection for that channel, and choose Select➡Inverse, and Filter➡Blur➡Gaussian Blur. Set the Radius to approximately 25.

7 Choose Select➡Inverse and Filter➡Blur➡Gaussian➡Blur again but use a slightly smaller radius this time. Try 8. This is what you're looking for.

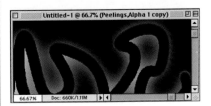

8 Choose Image➡Adjust➡Invert to invert the stripes.

9 Choose Duplicate Channel from the Channels palette menu. Choose New for the Document, name the new file (Peelings Channel), and click OK.

10 Save the new file that opened; then close it. This file will be used as a displacement map in Step 12. The blurred, gray edges causes the edges of the stripes to be distorted.

11 Return to the type layer (Peelings). Select→All and choose Filter→Distort→Displace. Set the Horizontal and Vertical Scale percentages both to 5 (Stretch to Fit, Repeat Edge Pixels).

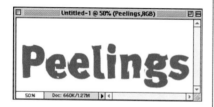

12 A new dialog box opens asking you to find a displacement map. Locate the file saved in Step 10 (Peelings Channel) and click Open. You see small distortions in the type. Deselect the selection.

13 Load the transparency selection from the type (Peelings) layer; then intersect that selection with the selection from the Alpha 1 channel.

14 Choose a second foreground color (CMYK: 20, 10, 70, 0) for the type and fill the selection. Deselect the selection.

15 Next, choose Filter➡Render➡ Lighting Effects. Select the Torn preset from the pop-up menu or match the settings seen here.

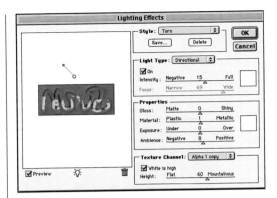

Click OK to see the effect.

16 And there you have it. To fine-tune the lighter color, I redid Step 13 to make a selection, added a little noise (Filter➡Noise➡Add Noise), and adjusted the color (Image➡Adjust➡Hue/Saturation). Always the shadow.

VARIATIONS

Adding texture to one of the colors helps separate the two parts (Meta Plus Black at 130 points). Load the transparency selection from the type layer and then subtract the selection from the Alpha 1 channel.

Choose Filter➡Texture➡ Texturizer. Use these settings: Canvas, Scaling: 135%, Relief: 10, Light: Top. ●

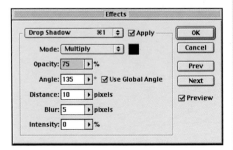

This classic effect has been made even easier with the new layer effects, and the technique described here gives you great control over the transparent box even after it has been created.

1 Open a file containing an image for the background. I used this one from Vivid Details (P5TM➡ Images➡Vivid Details➡MM_0028. TIF). Create a new layer (Layer 1) and use one of the selection tools to make a selection for the shape of the box.

2 Choose white for the foreground color and fill the selection. Then lower the Layer 1 Opacity to 50%. You might set the Opacity to any percentage that works—as long as it is light enough for the type to be read.

3 Choose Layer➡Effects➡Drop Shadow and choose settings for the shadow. Here is what I used.

And here is the result.

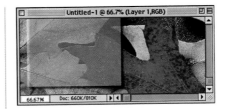

4 Choose Layer➡Effects➡Create Layer to put the drop shadow into a new layer below the white box.

5 Make the drop shadow layer active. The selection should still be active. Press Delete to clear the shadow away from underneath the white box. Deselect the selection.

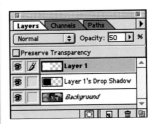

6 Link the two new layers by clicking in the box to the right of the eye next to the Layer 1 preview in the Layers palette. You can now use the Move tool to move the box around the image.

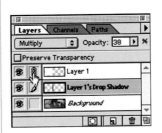

7 Of course, we need to add type. Make Layer 1 active and use the Type tool to enter the text (Adobe Garamond Regular at 12 points).

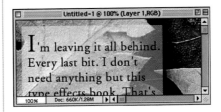

207

I'm leaving it all behind. Every last bit. I don't need anything but this type effects book. That's all I need in this world. What else is there really?

I'm leaving it all behind. Every last bit. I don't need anything but this type effects book. That's all I need in this world. What else is there really?

8 Also, you can adjust the whiteness of the box by using the Layer 1 Opacity slider. And you can darken or lighten the shadow by using the Opacity slider for the shadow layer. Here is the image after adjustments.

VARIATIONS

Color

For this variation, I filled the selection in Step 2 with a color (CMYK: 50, 25, 0, 0) instead of white and I used white type. I also added a drop shadow to the type layer after completing Step 8.

Transparent Type

Instead of making a box in Step 1, use the Type Mask tool to enter the text (Matrix Bold at 65 points). Complete the rest of the steps. This Vivid Details image is also on the CD-ROM (P5TM➡Images➡Vivid Details➡MM_0122.TIF).

Cut Out

After Step 2, deselect the selection and use the Type Mask tool to enter the text (Matrix at 65 points). Press Delete to clear the type from the box; then load the transparency selection of the current layer before finishing the rest of the steps. ●

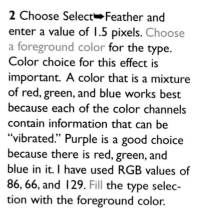

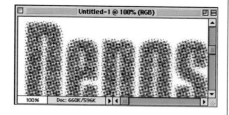

Applying filters to individual color channels makes these halftone dots vibrate.

1 Create a new file and then use the Type Mask tool to enter the text. (I used Compacta at 120 points.)

2 Choose Select➡Feather and enter a value of 1.5 pixels. Choose a foreground color for the type. Color choice for this effect is important. A color that is a mixture of red, green, and blue works best because each of the color channels contain information that can be "vibrated." Purple is a good choice because there is red, green, and blue in it. I have used RGB values of 86, 66, and 129. Fill the type selection with the foreground color.

3 While the type selection is still active, choose Filter➡Pixelate➡ Pointillize. This filter makes your image look like a pointillist painting. Enter a Cell size of 5 pixels.

4 Deselect the type and choose Filter➡Pixelate➡Color Halftone. Click on the Defaults button and enter a Max. Radius of 4 pixels.

5 Make only the Red channel active, and choose Filter➡ Pixelate➡Mosaic. Enter a cell size of 2 pixels. Then choose Filter➡Blur➡Gaussian Blur and enter a blur Radius of 0.5 pixels.

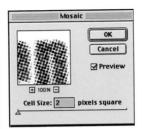

6 Make only the Green channel active and reapply the same filters used in Step 5, changing the Blur radius to 1.0 pixel.

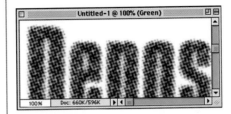

7 Finally, make only the Blue channel active and choose Filter➡ Pixelate➡Fragment.

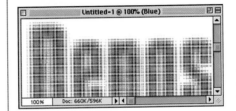

8 Return to the composite channel to view the finished type.

VARIATIONS

Instead of applying filters to each
channel, try moving the channels
independently. In Steps 5, 6, and 7,
choose Filter➡Other➡Offset
instead of applying the Mosaic, Blur,
and Fragment filters. Enter a different distance value each time you
offset a channel. For this example, I
set the Offset values for the Red
channel to -8 for both the Vertical
and Horizontal values. I skipped the
Green channel, and set both values
to 8 for the Blue channel.

For this effect, the Find Edges filter
was applied to the Red and Blue
channels only after completing
Steps 1 through 4. Do Step 8 to
complete the effect.

Try applying different filters to the
color channels. After step 5, with
only the Red channel active, choose
Filter➡Noise➡Dust & Scratches
and enter a Radius value of 10
and a Threshold value of 100.
Repeat for the Blue and Green
channels. ●

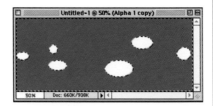

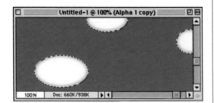

TOOLBOX

Water Droplets
(Lighting Effects
Style)

For the klutz in all of us, this basic effect is simple, but the enhancements are worth the extra steps.

1 Use the Type Mask tool to enter the text. I used Seagull Heavy at 65 points. Choose a foreground color for the type and fill the type. Because the type is only in the background for this effect, you can use any type (such as something created by another effect in this book) as long as the type image is merged into a single layer and has a nontransparent background.

2 Deselect the selection; then use the Elliptical Marquee tool to select a few oval shapes like you see here. These shapes will become the water droplets. The effect works best if you select ovals that run across the edge of the type. To select multiple areas as shown, simply hold down the Shift key as you drag each new selection. Save the selection as a new channel (Alpha 1).

3 Duplicate the Alpha 1 channel and make the new channel (Alpha 1 copy) the active channel. Choose Select➡Inverse to select the black area outside the white ovals. Change the foreground color to 50% gray and fill the selection.

4 Choose Select➡Inverse again to reselect the ovals. Choose Filter➡Blur➡Gaussian Blur. Blur the ovals slightly to add a little gray inside the edges. I set the radius at 5 pixels. Deselect the selection.

5 From the Channels palette menu, choose Duplicate Channel. Choose new from the Document pop-up menu and give the file a name (Water Droplet Displace).

6 A new file will pop up onscreen that is identical to the Alpha 1 channel. Save the file (Photoshop format) and close it.

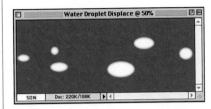

7 Return to the composite channel and the type layer. Choose Filter➡ Distort➡Displace. Use the settings shown here (Horizontal: 5%, Vertical: 5%, Stretch to Fit, Repeat Edge Pixels).

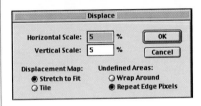

After you click OK, a dialog box asks you to find a file to use as a displacement map. Find and select the file that you saved in Step 6. Click Open to displace the water drops. You should see a slight distortion of the letters in the areas where you made the oval selections.

TIP If you want the type under the drops to be brighter than the rest of the type, load the selection from the Alpha I channel now.

215

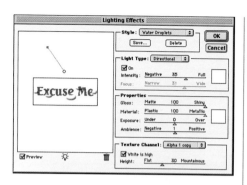

8 Choose Filter➡Render➡Lighting Effects. Load the Water Droplets preset or match the settings seen here.

9 Load the selection of the Alpha 1 channel; then choose Select➡Color Range. With the Eyedropper tool, click in the shadow area of one of the drops. Then use the Fuzziness slider to adjust the white areas in the preview so that most, but not all, of the shadows are selected. The Preview should look like this.

10 Choose Select➡Feather (2 pixels) to soften the selection. You will see the selection areas shrink slightly.

11 Change the foreground color to a light blue (CMYK: 30, 0, 0, 0). Fill the selection with the color to add a reflective highlight in the shadow areas.

12 Create a new layer (Layer 1), and load the selection from the Alpha 1 channel. Choose a foreground color for the drops (CMYK: 47, 0, 10, 0) and fill the selection with the color. Then change the layer blending mode to Multiply and lower the Opacity to around 90%. This adds color to the drops—but too much.

Choose Layer Options from the Layer palette pop-up menu. Hold the (Option) [Alt] key and drag the left half of the white marker underneath the Underlying bar to the left just slightly so that the light areas of the drops lighten.

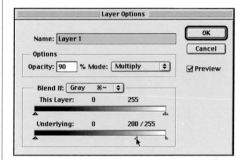

Bufflehead!

Wanna
Dance?

VARIATIONS

A Ripple

After Step 11, load the selection from the Alpha 1 channel, choose Select➦Modify➦Contract (4 pixels) Select➦Feather (3 pixels) to shrink and smooth the selection. Choose Filter➦Distort➦Ripple (Amount: 103%, Large). Vary the amount for the right effect.

Add Some Gloss

After Step 11, load the selection from the Alpha 1 channel, and choose Filter➦Artistic➦Plastic Wrap (8, 13, 11).

And a Reflection

Open an image file and copy the image. Close the file.

Create a new layer below Layer 1, and load the selection from the Alpha 1 channel. Paste the image into the selection, and choose Overlay from the layer blending mode menu. ●

Here's another effect that uses a displacement map and Lighting Effects filter in a one-two punch. In this effect, you load a file included on the CD-ROM, customize it for your type, and then use it for the distortions.

I Use the Type tool to enter the text into a new layer (I used Triplex at 135 points). Choose Layer➡ Type➡Render Layer.

2 Open the water rings displacement map file from the P5TM CD-ROM. Follow this path: P5TM➡ P5TM Files➡Displacement Maps➡Ring Displace.

3 Choose Select➡All and copy the image. Close the file.

4 Create a new channel (Alpha 1) in your type file, make it the active channel, and make the RGB channel visible.

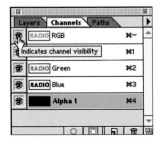

TOOLBOX

Ring Displace
(Displacement
Map)

Water Rings
(Lighting Effects
Style)

5 Paste in the image just copied.

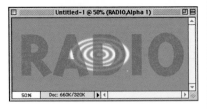

6 Now the rings must be resized to fit the type. Choose Edit➦ Transform➦Scale, and drag the box handles to resize the rings so they cover the area of the type that you want to be affected. This effect works best if the rings extend off of the type in the vertical direction as shown here. Press Return when satisfied.

7 Choose Duplicate Channel from the Channels palette menu. Select New from the Document menu and name the file (Radio Rings). Click OK to open the channel into a new image. Save the new file and close it.

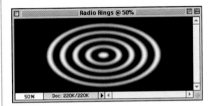

8 Return to the composite channel, make the Alpha I channel invisible, and deselect the selection.

9 Choose Filter➦Distort➦ Displace. Set both of the Scale percentages to 5 (Stretch to Fit, Repeat Edge Pixels).

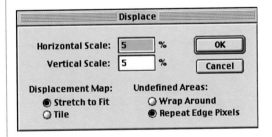

A dialog box opens asking you to find a displacement map. Find the file that you saved in Step 7 (Radio Rings). Click Open to distort the type.

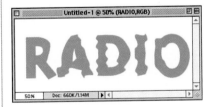

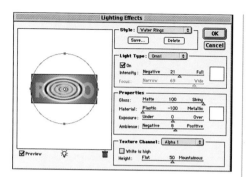

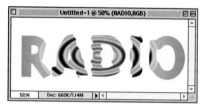

10 Choose Filter➥Render➥ Lighting Effects. Select Water Rings from the pop-up menu or match the settings seen here. You may need to adjust the Intensity so that the light doesn't wash out the color in your type. Also, make sure that the ring defining the light in the preview covers all of the type.

11 Now load the selection from the Alpha 1 channel and repeat Step 9.

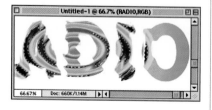

12 Deselect the selection and choose Select➥Color Range. Use the Eyedropper tool and click it in one of the shadow areas of the rings. Use the Fuzziness slider to adjust the selection (depicted by the white areas in the preview window) so that most, but not all, of the shadow areas are selected.

13 Choose Select➡Feather (4 pixels), and press Delete to reveal the layer below (just a white background for now).

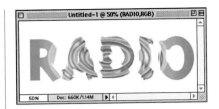

14 This effect needs a shadow to complete it. Choose Layer➡Effects➡Drop Shadow and try these settings: Multiply, Shadow Color: (CMYK: 95, 87, 28, 50), Opacity: 100%, Angle: 120°, Distance: 15, Blur: 16, Intensity: 0%.

15 To fine-tune the coloring, deselect the selection and choose Image➡Adjust➡Replace Color. Use the Eyedropper tool and the Fuzziness Slider as in Step 12 to select the areas of color you want to fix. I clicked the eyedropper on the outside edge of the "R." Here is the preview of the selection and the settings that I used to make the color more uniform throughout the image.

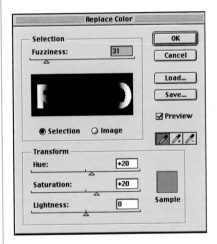

And the result.

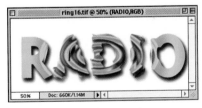

16 Finally, I added an outline to make the type edges a little more distinct. Create a new layer and move it below the type layer. Then load the transparency selection of the type layer. Choose a Foreground color that is close to the color of the type. Choose Edit➡Stroke (Centered, 2 pixels). ●

TOOLBOX

Blank Seal

Wax Seal (Lighting Effects Style)

Create a seal and a blob of wax, and smash them together using the Lighting Effects and Plastic Wrap filters to create the look of a wax-seal impression.

1 Creating the seal is the first step. It must be a black-and-white image that can be placed into a channel. I used Adobe Illustrator to make the generic image you see here. (It's on the CD-ROM if you want to use it: P5TM➡P5TM Files➡Blank Seal). In Step 2 type will be added. Copy the image and paste it into a new channel (Alpha 1) in a new RGB Photoshop file. Of course, you do not need to use an outline. You can simply use text if you want.

2 While in the Alpha 1 channel, use the Type tool to enter the text. This is Kabel at 25 points. If you are combining the type with an image, move the type into place within the image.

3 Create a new channel (Alpha 2), make it the active channel, and make the Alpha 1 channel visible. Use the Lasso tool to draw a blob that will define the shape of the wax. Choose Select➡Modify➡ Smooth (2 pixels) to smooth the selection drawn by that shaky hand of yours. Fill the selection with white.

4 Duplicate the Alpha 2 channel (Alpha 2 copy). Then load the selection from the Alpha 1 channel and press delete to fill it with black.

5 Load the selection of the active channel (Alpha 2 copy), and choose Filter➡Blur➡Gaussian Blur. Keep the blur setting low—all you want is a little grayness around the edges of the white areas. I set the Radius at 3 pixels.

6 Return to the composite channel and make a new layer (Layer 1). Load the selection from the Alpha 2 channel, set the foreground color to a color for the wax (CMYK: 0, 100, 100, 0), and fill the selection with the color.

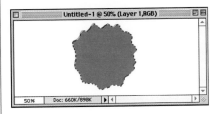

7 Next, choose Filter➡Render➡ Lighting Effects. Select the Wax Seal preset from the Style menu or match the settings seen in this figure.

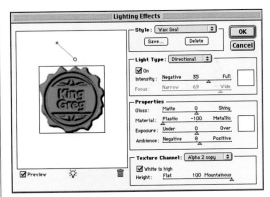

The wax raises.

8 Create a new layer (Layer 2) and move it below Layer 1. Make Layer 1 invisible.

9 The selection should still be active. Fill it with black.

10 Next, make Layer 1 the active layer, load the selection from the Alpha 1 channel, and cut the selection.

11 Make Layer 2 the active layer, make Layer 1 invisible, and paste in the selection just copied. A new layer (Layer 3) has been created. Choose Merge Down from the Layers palette to merge Layer 3 into Layer 2.

12 Choose Filter➡Blur➡Gaussian Blur. Set the Radius to about 2 pixels.

TIP If there are wide areas within the seal imprint, you might want to offset Layer 2. Make Layer 1 visible again, and grab the Move tool. Use the arrow keys to shift Layer 2 down and to the right a little.

13 Make Layer 1 visible again.

14 Make Layer I the active layer. Choose Filter➡Artistic➡Plastic Wrap. This filter adds a gloss to give the wax the right surface. Try these settings: Highlight Strength: 9, Detail: 9, Smoothness: 7. ●

WAVEMAP.dis
(displacement
map)

This effect is the very close cousin of the Potato Chips effect. The following technique uses the same displacement map to distort the shape of the edges.

1 Open the WAVEMAP.dis file from the P5TM CD-ROM (P5TM➡P5TM Files➡Displacement Maps➡ WAVEMAP.dis).

2 Choose Select➡All, copy the image, and close the file.

3 Create a new RGB file and create a new channel (Alpha 1). Paste in the image and deselect the selection.

4 Return to the composite channel and choose a foreground color for the waving type (CMYK: 0, 75, 100, 0). Then use the Type tool to enter the text (Compacta at 150 points). Choose Layer➡Type➡Render Layer.

5 Choose Filter➡Distort➡ Displacement Map (Horizontal Scale: 5%, Vertical Scale 5%, Stretch to Fit, Repeat edge pixels). Click OK.

Another dialog box opens asking you to find a displacement map. Find the file that you opened in Step 1 and click Open (P5TM CD-ROM➡P5TM Files➡Displacement Maps➡WAVEMAP.dis). This filter creates the waves around the edges of the type.

6 Load the selection from the Alpha 1 channel. This selection will be used to add highlights to the crests of the waving type. Choose New Adjustment Layer from the Layers palette menu. Turn on the Group With Previous Layer option, select Curves from the Type pop-up menu, and click OK to open the Curves dialog box. Grab the center of the diagonal line in the grid and bend the curve upward about this far.

Click OK to get this effect.

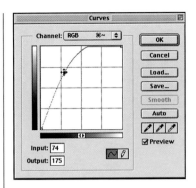

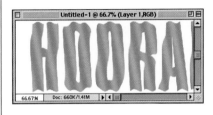

7 Create a new layer (Layer 1) for the shadow and move it below the type layer. The Layers palette should now look like this.

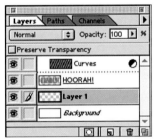

8 Load the transparency selection from the type layer; then subtract from that selection the selection from the Alpha 1 channel. Choose Select➡Feather (3 pixels). Choose black (or another color for the shadow) for the foreground color and fill the selection to create a shadow that turns darker as the wavy type dips down and lighter where it raises up. If you want to see it, temporarily make the type layer invisible. There's a little more work to do on the shadow.

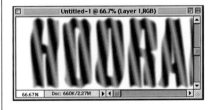

9 Load the transparency selection of the type layer, choose Select➡Feather (3 pixels), and feather the selection the same amount as in Step 8. Fill the selection with black; then choose Filter➡Fade Fill and lower the Opacity to 25%. Again, I temporarily made the type layer invisible to show you the shadow.

10 Deselect the selection. Select the Move tool and nudge the shadow down and to the right by using the arrow keys. I pressed each key three times.

VARIATIONS

Stripes
If you want to add stripes to the type, insert these three steps after Step 4.

1 Choose View➡Show Grid and make sure that the Snap to Grid option is turned on (View➡Snap to Grid). Choose File➡Preferences➡ Guides & Grid. The grid spacing determines the spacing of the stripes. I set the Gridline Every at one inch and the Subdivisions at 4.

2 Use the Rectangular Marquee tool to select one row in the grid. Drag the selection across the type; be careful to overlap both ends. Hold down the Shift key and make selections for every other row.

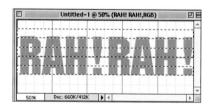

3 Choose a foreground color for the stripes (CMYK: 100, 75, 0, 0) and choose (Shift-Option-Delete) [Shift-Alt-Backspace] to fill the selection while preserving the layer transparency.

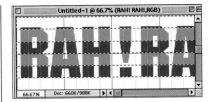

4 Deselect the selection and complete the rest of the steps (5 through 10).

Making Waves

If you want larger or smaller waves or have odd-sized type that won't work well with the displacement map on the CD-ROM, follow these steps to create your own displacement map.

1 Create a new file and create a new channel (Alpha 1). Choose View➡Show Grid and make sure that the Snap to Grid option is turned on (View➡Snap to Grid). Choose File➡Preferences➡Guides & Grid. The grid spacing determines the spacing of the stripes. I set the Gridline Every at one inch and the Subdivisions at 4. Here is the grid in the channel.

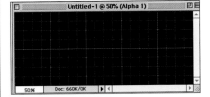

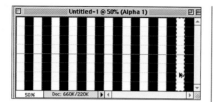

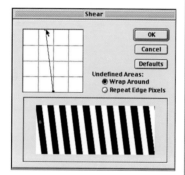

2 Use the Rectangular Marquee tool to select the first column. Choose white for the foreground color and fill the selection. Hold down (Command and Option) [Control and Alt]. Click on the selected column and drag it two columns to the right. Let go of the copied selection and repeat the copying until the entire channel is filled with stripes.

3 Deselect the selection and choose Filter➡Distort➡Shear. Turn on the Wrap Around option. Then grab the handle at the top of the line on the graph and move it to the left about as far as you see in this figure.

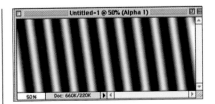

4 Click OK and choose Filter➡Blur➡Gaussian Blur (10 pixels). Blur the channel just enough so that the white in the stripes is no longer a strong white.

5 Choose Duplicate Channel from the Channels palette menu. In the dialog box that opens, choose New from the Document menu and name the new channel. The channel opens into a new file. Save the file (Photoshop format) and close it.

6 Proceed from Step 4 on page 228. In Step 5, use the file you just saved as the displacement map. ●

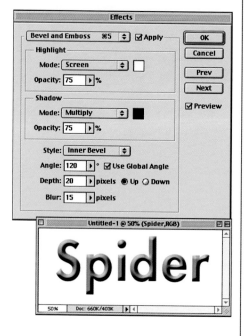

The new layer effects available in Photoshop 5.0 can help make some great effects like this one, which uses the Inner Bevel effect to add some dimension to a web that is spun by the Stained Glass filter.

1 Create a new file and use the Type tool to enter the text. (I used Futura Heavy at 100 points.)

2 Choose Layer➡Effects➡Bevel and Emboss. Select Inner Bevel as the Style, set the Depth to about 20 pixels, and raise the Blur amount enough to keep the type rounded (15 pixels).

3 Create a new layer (Layer 1) and load the transparency selection of the type layer. Choose Select→ Modify→Expand (1 pixel). Expanding this selection causes the lines of the web to stretch a little beyond the edges of the type, making it appear as if they wrap around the type.

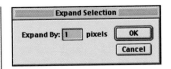

4 Choose white for the foreground color and fill the selection. Then press X to switch the foreground and background colors and choose a foreground color that will become the color of the web (CMYK: 0,100, 100, 40).

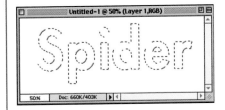

5 Choose Filter→Texture→Stained Glass. The Cell Size (10) determines the spacing in the web. The Border Thickness (4) determines the thickness of the lines. Set the Light Intensity to 0. Watch the preview to determine the best settings for your type.

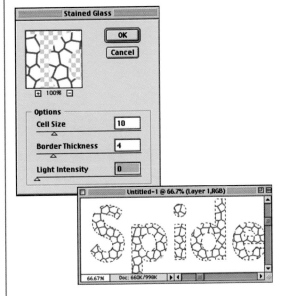

235

6 Deselect the selection and choose Select→Color Range. The colors that match the foreground color will automatically be selected. Raise the Fuzziness to the maximum (200) and click OK.

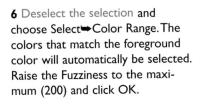

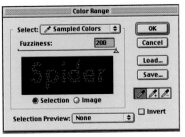

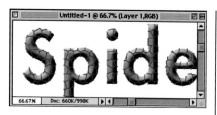

7 Choose Select➡Inverse and press Delete. Deselect the selection. Only the colored web lines should remain in this layer and you can see the underlying type again.

8 Choose Layer➡Effects➡Bevel and Emboss, and select the Inner Bevel style. Raise the Depth to about 10 pixels and set the Blur at 5 pixels. I also set the Opacity percentages for the shadows and highlights at 100% to raise the contrast in the raised web lines.

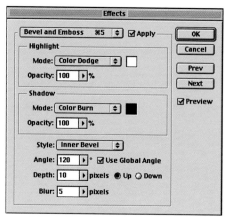

TIP **If the lines of the web do not appear to raise as they do in the figures here, the blur value may be too high.**

9 After adjusting the Bevel settings, go to the top of the dialog box and select Drop Shadow from the pop-up menu. Check the Apply box at the top. Create a slight shadow. I set the Distance and Blur both at 2 pixels. Click OK to apply the effects.

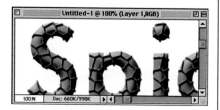

TIP **The benefit of using the layer effects to create special effects is that they are editable. To alter any of the settings, double-click on the "f" that appears next to the layer name in the Layers palette. The Effects dialog box opens.**

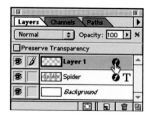

10 Finally, I used the Move tool to nudge the web layer up and to the left one keystroke each. I also added a drop shadow to the type layer.

VARIATIONS

Multiple Colors
Repeat Steps 3 through 8 to create another layer of webs. I repeated the steps once more to create a third layer of webs.

Sloppy Web
After Step 9, choose Filter➡Distort➡Ripple (150%, Medium) to create some sloppy lines.

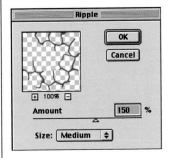

237

Silly String
Simply delete the type layer for this web only effect. There are four layers of webs in this example and they have all been rippled using slightly different settings. ●

Wet Cement
(Lighting Effects
Style)

In this effect, some surprising results are quickly produced by using the Diffuse filter to set up a texture channel for the Lighting Effects filter.

1 To begin this effect, a background image that looks something like cement is needed. Find your own or use the one provided on the P5TM CD-ROM (P5TM➡P5TM Files➡Images➡Cement).

2 Create a new channel (Alpha 1) and use the Type tool to enter the text. A handwritten typeface looks best, but anything works. I used Brush Stroke Fast at 55 points. Save the selection to create the Alpha 2 channel; then deselect the selection.

3 While still in the Alpha 1 channel, choose Filter➡Stylize➡Diffuse. Turn on the Lighten Only mode and click OK. Reapply this filter (Command-F) [Control-F] four or five times. The diffused edges grow a little more each time the filter is applied.

4 Load the selection of the Alpha 2 channel and choose Filter➡Blur➡ Gaussian Blur. I set the Radius at 5 pixels—just enough to lighten the inside edges of the type.

5 Choose Image➡Adjust➡Invert to invert the selection; then choose Image➡Adjust➡Brightness/ Contrast. Raise the Brightness to about 55 and the Contrast to 20.

6 Keep the selection active and add just a little bit of noise (Filter➡ Noise➡Add Noise; Amount: 5, Gaussian, Monochromatic). The noise will add a little texture inside the type. Deselect the selection.

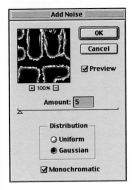

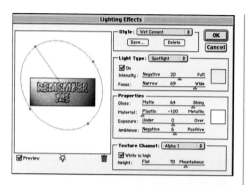

7 Return to the composite channel and choose Filter➡Render➡ Lighting Effects. Select the Wet Cement preset from the Style menu or match the settings seen here. The colored light that I included in this preset results in a good color for the cement, but if you don't like it, just click on the light color swatch to change it.

VARIATIONS

To get rid of the background, follow all of the preceding steps and then make the Alpha 1 channel active. Double-click on the Magic Wand tool to select it and bring the Magic Wand Options floating palette to the front. Set the tolerance to 1; then click the Magic Wand in the black area that surrounds the type. Choose Select➡Similar to make sure that all of the black areas are included in the selection. Return to the composite channel, and choose Select➡Modfiy➡Contract (2 pixels). Contract the selection enough so that the raised edges of the type are not included in the selection. Delete the selection and then deselect the selection. Finally, I added a drop shadow. ●

Appendix A

Contributors Listing

Filters

Alien Skin Software
1100 Wake Forest Rd. Suite 101
Raleigh, NC 27604
Phone: 919-832-4124
Fax: 919-832-4065

Black Box demo
Eye Candy 3.1 demo
Eye Candy for After Effects demo

Andromeda Software
699 Hampshire Rd. Suite 109
Thousand Oaks, CA 91361
Phone: 800-547-0055 or 805-379-4109
Fax: 805-379-5253
Orders@andromeda.com

3D Filter
Circular Multiple Images
Screens
Techture
Velociraptor

AutoFX
15 North Main Street. Suite 8
Wolfeboro, NH 03894
Phone: 603-569-8800
Fax: 603-569-9702

Photo/Graphic Edges demo
Photo/Graphic Patterns demo
Typo/Graphic Edges demo
Ultimate Texture Collection

MetaTools, Inc.
6303 Carpinteria Ave.
Carpinteria, CA 93013
805-566-6200
metasales@aol.com

Kai's Power Tools demo

Fonts

Delve Media Arts
P.O. Box 641053
San Francisco, CA 94164-1053
Phone: 415-474-0702
http:www.delvemediaarts.com

(PC only)

Fonthead Design
20942 Estada Lana
Bola Raton, FL 33433
http://www.fonthead.com
Fax: 561-482-3630

Foundry Group
Jon Armstrong
C/O FoundryGroup/Saiph Corporation
250 West 57th Street
New York, NY 10107
Phone: 718-384-2583
Jon@saiph.com

Garage Fonts
P.O. Box 3101
Del Mar, CA 92014
Phone: 619-755-3913
Fax: 619-755-4761
Info@garagefonts.com
http://www.garagefonts.com

Ingrimayne Type
Robert Schenk
P.O. Box 404
Rensselaer, IN 47979
Bobs@kagi.com
http://ingrimayne.saintjoe.edu/

Omnibus Typographi
Box 135
S-135 23 Tyreso
Sweden
Phone: +46 8 742 8336
Fax: +46 8 712 3993

P22 Type Foundry
P.O. Box 770 West Side Station
Buffalo, NY 14213-0070
Phone: 716-885-4490
Fax: 716-885-4482
P22@p22.com
http://www.p22.com

Snyder Shareware Fonts
1797 Ross Inlet Road
Coos Bay, OR 97420
Snyderrp@mail.coos.or.us

Synstelien Design
1338 North 120th Plaza, Apt# 9
Omaha, NE 68154
Phone: 402-491-3065
http://www.synfonts.com

Three Islands Press
P.O. Box 442
Rockland, ME 04841-0442
Phone: 207-596-6768
Fax: 207-596-7403
Info@3ip.com
http://www.3ip.com

Vintage Type
5662 Calle Real. #146
Goleta, CA 93117-2317

Vitatype Digital Fonts   **(PC only)**
5204 Hadley Court. #1
Overland Park, KS 66202
Phone: 913-677-2533
Jeff@vitatype.com
http://www.primenet/~jeffib

Images

D'Pix Division of Amber Productions, Inc.
41 W. Fourth Ave.
Columbus, OH 43201
Phone: 614-299-7192
Fax: 614-294-0002

Digital Stock
400 S. Sierra Ave. Suite 100
Solana Beach, CA 92075
Phone: 619-794-4040 or 800-545-4514
Fax: 619-794-4041

FotoSets
4104 24th Street. #425
San Francisco, CA 94114
Phone: 415-621-2061
Fax: 415-621-2917

Image Club Graphics
729 24th Ave. SE
Calgary, AB, Canada
T2G 5K8
Phone: 403-262-8008 or 800-661-9410
Fax: 403-261-7013
http://www.adobe.com/imageclub

Jawai Interactive
501 E. Fourth St. #511
Austin, TX 78701
Phone: 512-469-0502
Jawai@aol.com

Photo24 Texture Resource
7948 Faust Ave.
West Hills, CA 91304
Phone: 818-999-4184 or 800-582-9492
Fax: 818-999-5704
http://www.photo24.com

PhotoDisc/CMCD
2013 Fourth Ave. 4th Floor
Seattle, WA 98121
Phone: 206-441-9355 or 800-528-3472
http://www.photodisc.com

Software

Adobe Systems, Inc.
345 Park Avenue
San Jose, CA 95110-6000
Phone: 408-563-6000
Fax: 408-537-6000

Acrobat Reader 3.0 demo
After Effects 3.1 demo
Dimensions 3.0 demo
Illustrator 7.0 demo
Streamline 4.0 demo

Earthlink
Earthlink ISP
3100 New York Drive
Pasadena, CA 91107
Phone: 626-296-2400
Sales@earthlink.net

Macromedia
600 Townsend
San Francisco, CA 94103
Phone: 415-252-2000
http://www.macromedia.com

Shockwave r10
Fontographer 4.1 demo
FreeHand 8.0 demo
XRes 2.0 demo

Netscape
Phone: 650/937-3777
http://www.netscape.com

Navigator 4.04

Appendix B

What's on the CD-ROM

The CD-ROM included with this book contains many files that can help you create great type effects with stock images for you to use, demo versions of Photoshop plug-ins, and popular software applications. You can also find many of the type images that are on the pages of this book. Some of the techniques in this book use specially prepared files. All these files are on the CD-ROM.

Finally, on the CD-ROM are actions that you can load into the Photoshop Actions palette and use to create some of the same effects that you see in this book with a click of the mouse.

The CD-ROM is readable on both Macintosh and Windows platforms.

The CD-ROM includes six folders: Filters, Fonts, Images, P5TM Files, and Software. The following is a brief description of the folder contents.

Filters

Inside the Filters folder are four folders that contain different filters for use with Adobe Photoshop. Each folder represents a different company with varying numbers of filters from each. To use any of these plug-ins, they need to be copied into the Plug-ins folder inside the Adobe Photoshop 5.0 folder on your hard drive. Follow this path to copy the files: Adobe Photoshop 5.0➡Plug-ins. The next time you start Photoshop, these third-party plug-in demos appear at the bottom of the Filter menu, as shown in this figure.

Fonts

The CD-ROM offers fourteen different folders within the Fonts folder, each from a company supplying the fonts, including over 30 different fonts and several different formats. Please note the instructions provided with each company's product for information on shareware conditions, installation, and purchasing.

Images

Inside the Images folder are seven folders that contain a variety of low, medium, and high-resolution stock photography images. Many of the images contain textures and backgrounds that you can use to make great-looking type. Most likely, you will decide to keep these images on the CD-ROM where you can access them at will—without having them eat up memory on your hard drive. (If you want, you can also move them to your hard drive.) You can open all these images with the Open command in Adobe Photoshop.

P5TM Files

There are several folders within this folder. With one exception (the Lighting Styles folder), all of the files within these folders can be left on the CD-ROM and accessed when directed in the instruction steps. If you want, you can also place them in any folder on your hard drive that you don't plan on forgetting about.

Lighting Styles

There are 21 Lighting Style presets that you can use with Photoshop's Lighting Effects filter. These are the only files within the P5TM Files folder that must be copied to your hard drive in order to be useable. Proper installation of these files is critical. In order to use these files, they must be copied from the CD-ROM into the Lighting Styles folder within the Adobe Photoshop folder on your hard drive. Follow this path to find the proper folder: Adobe Photoshop 5.0➡Plug-ins➡Filters➡Lighting FX➡Lighting Styles. After copying these files, the next time you start Photoshop, they will appear in the Style list in the Lighting Effects dialog box.

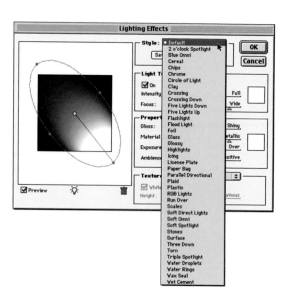

248

Actions

There are 31 actions in the action set that enable you to create some of the same effects in this book with a click of a button. To load the actions into the Actions palette, choose Load Actions from the Actions palette menu. Follow this path to find the P5TM Actions file: P5TM➡P5TM Files➡Actions➡P5TM Actions.

The actions are divided into two groups. In order to run the first group, you must first use the Type Mask tool to enter the text; then click on the name of the effect you want to apply and choose Play from the Actions palette menu. To use the actions in the second group, use the Type tool to enter the text before playing the action.

These actions were optimized for 150dpi files. Results might vary depending on the specific characteristics of the files you use. After you load these actions, you can alter them to suit you needs. To learn more about actions and how to modify them, consult your Photoshop 5.0 User's Manual.

Software

Inside this folder are demo versions of popular software applications that you can try. For detailed information about how to install and run these applications, consult the READ ME files contained within the individual folders. Each folder contains an installation file that walks you through the installation of the software.

Gallery

page 22

page 44

page 28

page 50

page 34

page 56

page 40

page 58

Distressed

page 62

page 78

ELEPHANT

page 66

page 84

page 68

page 90

page 74

Halftone

page 98

Highlights

MARBLE

PAPER BAG

Patterns

NEON

page 134

page 152

page 138

page 156

page 142

page 160

page 146

page 166

VIBRATION

page 210

page 228

Water Droplets

page 214

page 234

Water Rings

page 220

page 238

page 224